MATH PHONICS™
ADDITION & SUBTRACTION

BONUS BOOK–ALL NEW IDEAS

Quick Tips and Alternative Techniques for Math Mastery

BY MARILYN B. HEIN

ILLUSTRATED BY RON WHEELER

Teaching & Learning Company

1204 Buchanan St., P.O. Box 10
Carthage, IL 62321-0010

THIS BOOK BELONGS TO

_____

ACKNOWLEDGEMENTS

Special thanks to Regina Cortner, Mary Gallagher, Taylor Padgett, Jed and Todd Shepherd and Cheyenne Truelove for field testing games and worksheets. I am also very grateful for the support given to me by Karen Zajkowski, Sue Wilkey, Wesley Learned, Amy McEachern, Cindy Goodwin and Kay Suchan.

DEDICATION

I dedicate this book to my mother and father, Vincent and Cleora Vestring and my mother-in-law and father-in-law, Roman and Barbara Hein all of whom have passed away since I began writing the Math Phonics™ series. All four of them valued education very, very highly and for this we can never thank them enough!

Cover art by Ron Wheeler

Copyright © 2002, Teaching & Learning Company

ISBN No. 1-57310-345-4

Printing No. 987654321

Teaching & Learning Company
1204 Buchanan St., P.O. Box 10
Carthage, IL 62321-0010

The purchase of this book entitles teachers to make copies for use in their individual classrooms only. This book, or any part of it, may not be reproduced in any form for any other purposes without prior written permission from the Teaching & Learning Company. It is strictly prohibited to reproduce any part of this book for an entire school or school district, or for commercial resale.

All rights reserved. Printed in the United States of America.

Math Phonics™ is a registered trademark to Marilyn B. Hein.

TABLE OF CONTENTS

What Is Math Phonics™? 5
How Was Math Phonics™ Developed? 5
What Are the Principles of Math Phonics™? 6
How to Make Movable Number Lines 7
Summary of the 10 Basic Steps 8
Lesson Plan 1: Demonstrating Ruler Addition–Pairs for 11 & 12 9
   Counting Line 11
   Rainbow Activities 12
   Worksheet A—Number Pairs for 11 & 12 ... 14
   Worksheet B—More Practice for 11 & 12 ... 15
   Worksheet C—Connect the Dots 16
Lesson Plan 2: Pairs for 13 & 14 17
   Four-Part Rainbow Activities 18
   Worksheet D—Number Pairs for 13 & 14 ... 20
   Worksheet E—More Practice for 13 & 14 ... 21
   Worksheet F—Math Art 22
Lesson Plan 3: Pairs for 15, 16, 17 & 18 23
   Addition Facts Chart 25
   T-Tables 29
   Worksheet G—Number Pairs for 15-18 ... 32
   Worksheet H—More Practice for 15-18 ... 33
   Worksheet I—Math Maze 34
Lesson Plan 4: Three-Way Flash Cards 35
   Three-Way Flash Cards 36
   Worksheet J—Addition Review 40
   Worksheet K—Number Pairs–Subtraction Practice 41
   Worksheet L—Crossword Puzzle 42
Lesson Plan 5: Subtraction–11 & 12 as Minuends 43
   Worksheet M—11 & 12 as Minuends 44
   Worksheet N—11 & 12 as Minuends 45
   Worksheet O—Math Weave 46
Lesson Plan 6: Subtraction–13 & 14 as Minuends 47

Worksheet P—13 & 14 as Minuends 48
Worksheet Q—Practice! 11-14 as Minuends 49
Subtraction Stepping-Stones 50
Lesson Plan 7: Subtraction–15-18 as Minuends 51
   Worksheet R—15-18 as Minuends 52
   Worksheet S—15-18 as Minuends 53
   Worksheet T—Brain-Powered Elevator! 54
   Worksheet U—Subtraction Review 55
Lesson Plan 8: Regrouping in Subtraction ... 56
   Play Money 57
   Worksheet V—Regroup & Subtract 60
   Worksheet W—Regroup & Subtract 61
   Worksheet X—Regroup & Subtract 62
   Worksheet Y—Regroup & Subtract 63
Lesson Plan 9: A Gaggle of Great Ideas 64
Poster Idea Example—Facts of the Week 68
   Homework Passes/Prize Coupons 69
   Worksheet Z—Calendar Math 70
   Worksheet AA—Treasure Trove 71
   Worksheet BB—Adding & Subtracting 2s & 4s 72
   Even/Odd Number Lines 73
   Hopscotch Numbers 74
   Nines Game Cards 81
   Solitaire Cards 82
   Number Neighbor Flash Cards 87
Lesson Plan 10: Rules, Games & Assessments 91
   Assessment–Addition & Subtraction 11-18 ... 92
   Assessment–Addition & Subtraction 93
Base 10 Counting Chart 94
Answer Key 95

Dear Teacher or Parent,

I still love math! I guess it shows. The father of one of my tutorial students recently told me, "You're the first one who has made math fun for our son! I had a great time writing *Math Phonics™–Addition* and *Math Phonics™–Subtraction*. Now I find myself with a whole notebook full of new ideas for demonstrating and drilling addition and subtraction basic facts. The result is this *Math Phonics™–Addition & Subtraction Bonus Book*. Everything is new–demonstrations, worksheets, activity sheets, games–even the flash cards and fact charts are new!

This book builds on the original addition and subtraction books and focuses mostly on the problems involving numbers in the teens–the ones kids can't count out on their fingers! Don't skip the original books. They have many great ideas which are not repeated here.

This book is ideal for a year-end review of addition and subtraction, or use all three books throughout the year. This bonus book is also perfect for middle school students who need a review, or for adult education, home schooling and tutoring. Teachers in all of those areas have reviewed the Math Phonics™ materials and given them a thumbs up.

One last thought–some students can get the right answers in addition and subtraction problems, but they get them by counting out the answers mentally or on their fingers. (My 20-something son, Robert, remembers that a girl got into trouble in the second grade for counting out answers on her teeth!) Everybody has to count something out from time to time, but students really need to memorize most of the math facts to survive in the problems which have several steps like fractions or algebra. If you stop in the middle of a problem like that to count something out, you lose your place in the logic of the problem and have to start over. I think this is a common reason that some people crash and burn when they get to fractions or simply can't learn algebra.

So please take a look. I think you'll like the materials in this bonus book. You might even find some reluctant students who will find that math is fun!

Sincerely,

Marilyn

Marilyn B. Hein

WHAT IS MATH PHONICS™?

Math Phonics™ is a specially designed program for teaching addition and subtraction facts initially or for remedial work.

WHY IS IT CALLED MATH PHONICS™?

In reading, phonics is used to group similar words, and it teaches the students simple rules for pronouncing each word.

In *Math Phonics*™, math facts are grouped and learned by means of simple patterns, rules and mnemonic devices.

In reading, phonics develops mastery by repetitive use of words already learned.

Math Phonics™ uses drill and review to reinforce students' understanding.

HOW WAS MATH PHONICS™ DEVELOPED?

Why did "Johnny" have so much trouble learning to read during the years that phonics was dropped from the curriculum of many schools in this country? For the most part, he had to simply memorize every single word in order to learn to read, an overwhelming task for a young child. If he had an excellent memory or a knack for noticing patterns in words, he had an easier time of it. If he lacked those skills, learning to read was a nightmare, often ending in failure—failure to learn to read and failure in school.

Phonics seems to help many children learn to read more easily. Why? When a young child learns one phonics rule, that one rule unlocks the pronunciation of dozens or even hundreds of words. It also provides the key to parts of many larger words. The trend in U.S. schools today seems to be to include phonics in the curriculum because of the value of that particular system of learning.

As a substitute teacher, I have noticed that math teacher manuals sometimes have some valuable phonics-like memory tools for teachers to share with students to help them memorize math facts—the addition, subtraction, multiplication and division facts which are the building blocks of arithmetic. However, much of what I remembered from my own education was not contained in the available materials. I decided to create my own materials based upon what I had learned during the past 40 years as a student, teacher and parent.

The name *Math Phonics*™ occurred to me because the rules, patterns and memory techniques that I have assembled are similar to language arts phonics in several ways. Most of these rules are short and easy to learn. Children are taught to look for patterns and use them as "crutches" for coming up with the answer quickly. Some groups have similarities so that learning one group makes it easier to learn another. Last of all, *Math Phonics*™ relies on lots of drill and review, just as language arts phonics does.

Children *must* master addition, subtraction, multiplication and division facts and the sooner the better. When I taught seventh and eighth grade math over 20 years ago, I was amazed at the number of students who had not mastered the basic math facts. At that time, I had no idea how to help them. My college math classes did not give me any preparation for that situation. I had not yet delved into my personal memory bank to try to remember how I had mastered those facts.

When my six children had problems in that area, I was strongly motivated to give some serious thought to the topic. I knew my children had to master math facts, and I needed to come up with additional ways to help them. For kids to progress past the lower grades without a thorough knowledge of those facts would be like trying to learn to read without knowing the alphabet.

I have always marveled at the large number of people who tell me that they "hated math" when they were kids. I wonder how many of them struggled with the basic math facts when they needed to have them clearly in mind. I firmly believe that a widespread use of Math Phonics™ could be a tremendous help in solving the problem of "math phobia."

WHAT ARE THE PRINCIPLES OF MATH PHONICS™?

There are three underlying principles of Math Phonics™.
They are: 1. Understanding
           2. Learning
           3. Mastery
Here is a brief explanation of the meaning of these principles.

1. **UNDERSTANDING:** All true mathematical concepts are abstract which means they can't be touched. They exist in the mind. For most of us, understanding such concepts is much easier if they can be related to something in the real world—something that can be touched.

   Thus I encourage teachers and parents to have students find answers for themselves using small objects, number lines and counting charts. I think this helps the students to remember answers once they have discovered them on their own.

2. **LEARNING:** Here is where the rules and patterns mentioned earlier play an important part. A child can be taught a simple rule and on the basis of that, call to mind a whole set of math facts. But the learning necessary for the addition, subtraction, multiplication and division facts must be firmly in place so that the information will be remembered next week, next month and several years from now. That brings us to the next principle.

3. **MASTERY:** We have all had the experience of memorizing some information for a test or quiz tomorrow and then promptly forgetting most of it. This type of memorization will not work for the math facts. In order for children to master these facts, Math Phonics™ provides visual illustrations, wall charts, flash cards, practice sheets, worksheets and games. Some students may only need one or two of these materials, but there are plenty from which to choose for those who need more.

HOW TO MAKE MOVABLE NUMBER LINES

Just as the Base 10 Counting Chart (page 94) is an excellent aid in teaching multiplication and division, the movable number line is an outstanding way to demonstrate addition and subtraction facts.

Here are variations that you can use for different situations.

1. CLASSROOM DEMONSTRATIONS WITH MAGNETIC CHALKBOARD

MATERIALS
18 plastic container lids or laminated index cards

black permanent marker or black vinyl stick-on letters

one roll of magnetic tape—sold at school supply stores and variety stores. Can be cut with scissors and pressed onto the back side of the lids.

STEP 1
On the blank sides of the plastic container lids, or index cards write or press the numerals 1-18, one on each lid or card.

STEP 2
Cut pieces of the magnetic tape about 3/4" long, remove the protective paper and press onto the back side of the lids or cards.

STEP 3
Place the lids or cards in numeric order along the top of the magnetic chalkboard and use as directed in the lesson plans of this book.

(Without a magnetic chalkboard, punch a hole in the top of each lid or card. Put a curtain ring through the hole and hang the lids or cards from a dowel or curtain rod. Attach the curtain rod or dowel to the wall with brackets.)

2. DEMONSTRATION TO ONE STUDENT

MATERIALS
18 poker chips or similar-shaped objects
18 small round white pressure sensitive stickers
roll of magnetic tape
jelly roll pan or cookie sheet with raised edges

STEP 1
Place a round white sticker in the center of each poker chip.

STEP 2
Place a 3/4" piece of magnetic tape on the other side of each poker chip.

STEP 3
Write numerals 1-18, one on each chip.

STEP 4
Assemble the poker chips on the cookie sheet and use as directed in the lesson plans in this book.

NOTE: See Lesson Plan 1 on page 9 for instructions on how to use students as a movable number line.

SUMMARY OF THE 10 BASIC STEPS

1. **Demonstrating Ruler Addition–Pairs for 11 & 12**

   This step will introduce using the ruler to find number pairs for given sums–in this case 11 and 12.

2. **Pairs for 13 & 14**

   The same methods will be used to practice addition facts in which the sum is 13 or 14.

3. **Pairs for 15, 16, 17 & 18**

   This is one last set of materials for practicing facts in which the answer is 15, 16, 17 or 18.

4. **Three-Way Flash Cards**

   This is the transitional step showing students how to make subtraction problems from addition problems. Three-way flash cards reinforce this idea.

5. **Subtraction–11 & 12 as Minuends**

   This step introduces subtraction using ruler addition number pairs.

6. **Subtraction–13 & 14 as Minuends**

   Again, addition number pairs are used in practicing subtraction.

7. **Subtraction–15, 16, 17 & 18 as Minuends**

   One last set of materials is provided for practicing these last four groups of subtraction facts.

8. **Regrouping in Subtraction**

   These materials give students a concrete way of understanding regrouping (or borrowing) in subtraction.

9. **A Gaggle of Great Ideas**

   This step contains seven miscellaneous ideas–everything from games to flash cards and a classroom contest.

10. **Rules, Games & Assessments**

    This step contains a summary of rules and games from the other nine steps and two assessment pages.

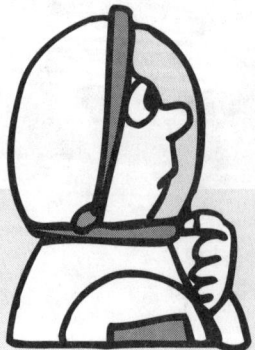

LESSON PLAN 1: ADDITION—11 & 12

OBJECTIVE: Show students an easy way to memorize number pairs for 11 and 12. (For this demonstration, number pairs for 11 will be used. Any other group can be explained the same way.)

MATERIALS: wall-size movable number line using counters 1 through 11 or 11 students lined up at the front of the room. This lesson plan will be written for using the students. Laminated ruler-sized counting line or 12-inch ruler for each student (page 11), rainbow activity pages (pages 12-13), worksheets (pages 14-16)

DEMONSTRATION: Arrange students or numbers on a movable number line as shown above. Ask the rest of the class to make an addition fact about the students and write on the board: 1 + 10 = 11

Now have one of the students move from the right to the left and again ask for an addition fact:

Below the first fact write: 2 + 9 = 11

Next have another student move from right to left and ask for the addition fact:

Below the first two facts write: 3 + 8 = 11

Have one more student move from the right to the left and ask for that addition fact:

4 + 7 = 11

Have one last student move from the right to the left and write the last fact:

5 + 6 = 11

LESSON PLAN 1: CONTINUED

You should now have this set of facts on the board:

1 + 10 = 11
2 + 9 = 11
3 + 8 = 11
4 + 7 = 11
5 + 6 = 11

Give each student a ruler-sized number line (page 11). Now have the students find 1 and 10 on the ruler-sized number line by putting their left index finger below the 1 and their right index finger below the 10. Next, have them find the next number pair by moving each finger one number toward the center and say that number pair. Continue until they have reached 5 + 6.

Point out to students that the numbers in the left column are getting larger each time and the numbers in the center column are getting smaller each time. Students should be able to give number pairs without the ruler after a little practice. (Note: Always put the smaller number on the left so that numbers are being given in the left to right order that they are on the ruler.)

HANDOUT: Give each student two copies of page 12. Show them how to make a "rainbow" of number pairs for 11–see page 13 for an illustration. After making the rainbow, they list the number pairs at the top of the page.

If necessary, repeat the process for the number pairs for 12.

CLASSROOM DRILL: Have the class give you the number pairs one at a time for each group. For the 11s, write on the board: 1 + 10 = 11.

Write the 2 under the 1 and ask for the next pair. Write the rest of that fact. Write the 3 under the 2 and ask for the next pair. Continue.

Have the class chant the entire group in unison while looking at the list.

1 + 10 = 11
2 + 9 = 11
3 + 8 = 11
4 + 7 = 11
5 + 6 = 11

Now cover the list and have the class chant the number pairs again.

Repeat for the 12s.

WORKSHEETS: The lower group of problems on Worksheet A is practice for subtraction. For Worksheet B, have students do the first problem. Then count out the next problem on a base 10 counting chart (page 94). Show them that they can regroup the one group of 10 into the 10s column. That is easier than using a counting chart. The problems are in groups of four with each one having the same answer in the 1s place. (Note: Refer to pages 82-83 in *Math Phonics™–Addition* for additional worksheets to practice these facts.)

If you are using this as a review for your students, use the notes on page 88 in *Math Phonics™–Addition* and page 15 in *Math Phonics™–Subtraction*.

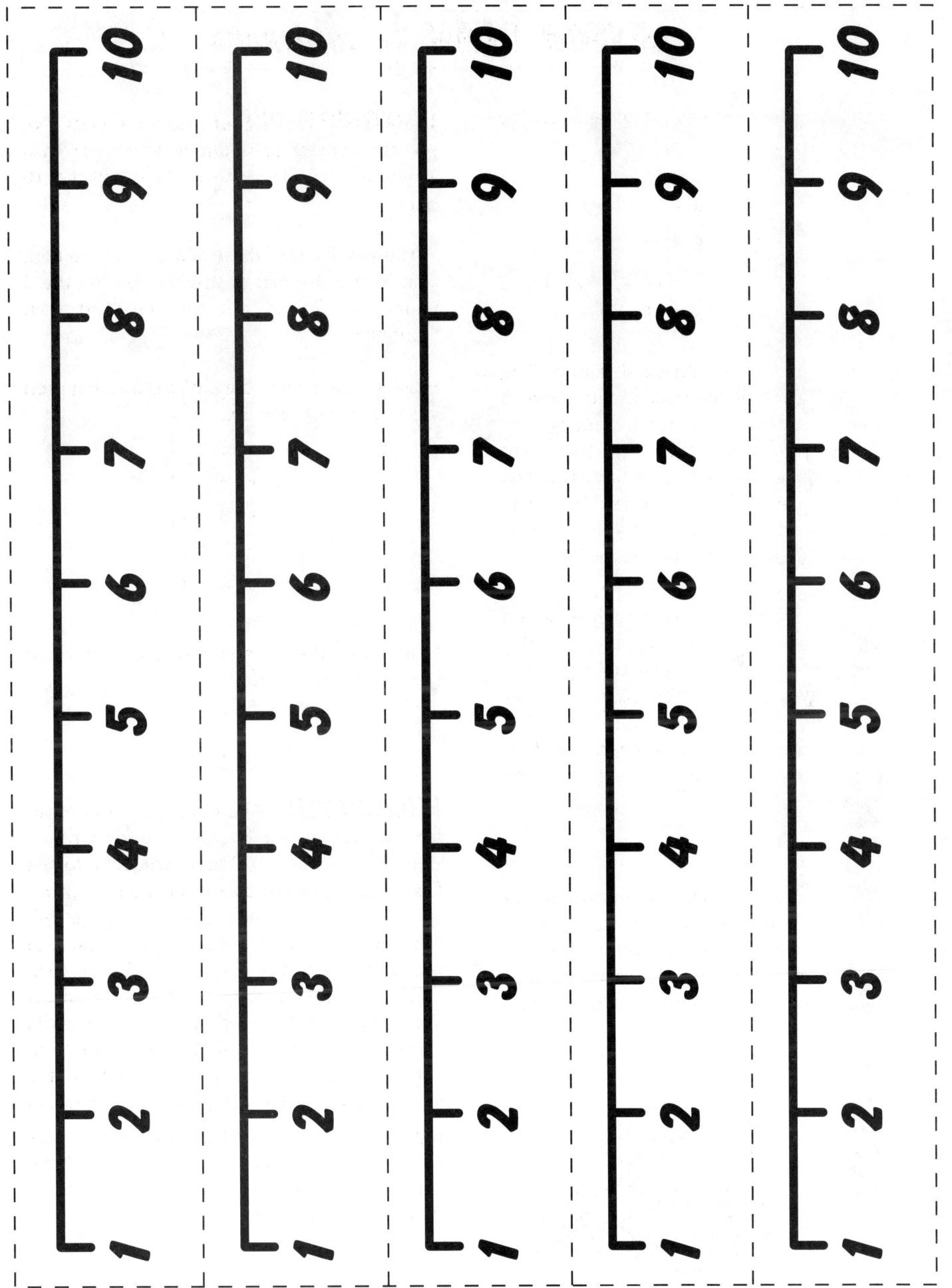

Name _____

NUMBER PAIRS FOR ____

1　2　3　4　5　6　7　8　9　10

NUMBER PAIRS FOR 11

1 + 10
2 + 9
3 + 8
4 + 7
5 + 6

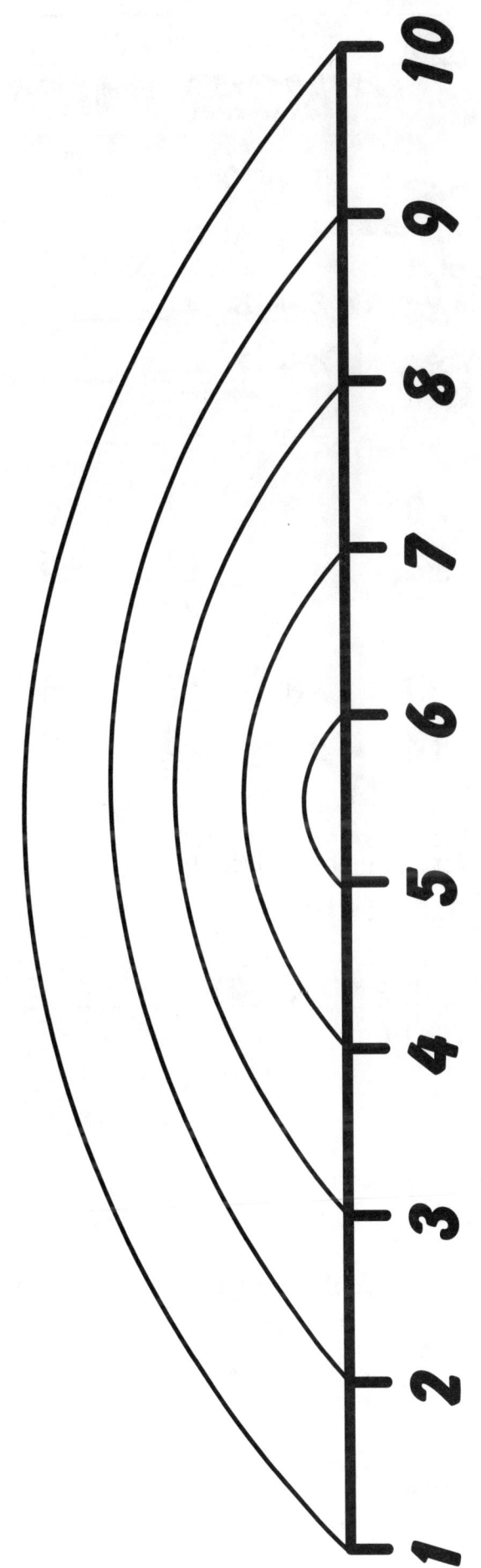

Name _____   WORKSHEET A

NUMBER PAIRS FOR 11 & 12

1 + 10 = ____   2 + 10 = ____
2 + 9 = ____   3 + 9 = ____
3 + 8 = ____   4 + 8 = ____
4 + 7 = ____   5 + 7 = ____
5 + 6 = ____   6 + 6 = ____

1. 10   9   8   7   6   5   4   3   2   1
    +1   +2   +3   +4   +5   +6   +7   +8   +9   +10

2. 10   9   8   7   6   5   4   3   2
    +2   +3   +4   +5   +6   +7   +8   +9   +10

Fill in the missing numbers. Use the problems above if you need help.

3. ☐   ☐   ☐   ☐   ☐   ☐   ☐   ☐
    +8   +3   +4   +7   +9   +2   +6   +5
    11   11   11   11   11   11   11   11

4. ☐   ☐   ☐   ☐   ☐   ☐   ☐
    +9   +3   +5   +7   +6   +8   +4
    12   12   12   12   12   12   12

5. You are in charge of the classroom supplies. If you sold 8 pencils on Monday and 4 pencils on Tuesday, how many did you sell in all? _____

6. If you sold 7 packs of notebook paper and 4 packs of graph paper, what is the total number of packs of paper sold? _____

CHALLENGE:
Look at the front page of today's paper. On the back of this worksheet, list all the ways numbers are used.

Name _____   **WORKSHEET B**

MORE PRACTICE FOR 11s & 12s

1.	6	25	36	56	7	34	64	87
	+5	+6	+5	+5	+4	+7	+7	+4

2.	8	23	58	88	9	42	72	89
	+3	+8	+3	+3	+2	+9	+9	+2

3.	8	38	44	54	7	25	47	65
	+4	+4	+8	+8	+5	+7	+5	+7

4.	9	29	43	83	6	56	76	86
	+3	+3	+9	+9	+6	+6	+6	+6

Write the number pairs. Start with a number plus 10.

11	12	13	14
___ + 10	___ + 10	___ + 10	___ + 10
___ + ___	___ + ___	___ + ___	___ + ___
___ + ___	___ + ___	___ + ___	___ + ___
___ + ___	___ + ___	___ + ___	___ + ___
___ + ___	___ + ___		

5. You noticed that 23 blue pens and 8 red pens had been sold. How many pens were sold in all? _____

6. You received two shipments of pencils. One had 14 boxes of pencils and the other had 7 boxes of pencils. What was the total number of boxes of pencils received by the class? _____

CHALLENGE:
I'm thinking of a number. When you add 7 to my number, the answer is 11. What is the number? _____

Name _____   **WORKSHEET C**

CONNECT THE DOTS

Write in the correct answers. Connect the dots between problems with the same answer.

8 + 4 = ____   3 + 2 = ____

6 + 5 = ____   3 + 3 = ____

8 + 2 = ____   5 + 2 = ____

7 + 2 = ____   4 + 4 = ____

5 + 3 = ____   6 + 3 = ____

3 + 4 = ____   5 + 5 = ____

2 + 4 = ____   7 + 4 = ____

4 + 1 = ____   9 + 3 = ____

LESSON PLAN 2: ADDITION—13 & 14

OBJECTIVE: Give students addition practice with number pairs for 13 and 14.

REVIEW: Have students chant number pairs for 11 and 12. Continue this each day until students have them memorized. Have a class aid or parent volunteer check each student to see if each one can say these number pair groups.

MATERIALS: movable number line, ruler-sized number lines (page 11), four-part rainbow activity pages (pages 18-19) (vinyl page protectors and markers could be used so that pages could be used more than once.), worksheets (pages 20-22)

DEMONSTRATION: Have students find number pairs for 13 using a movable number line, students or the ruler-sized number lines and write them on the board. Do the same for 14.

HANDOUT: Give each student a four-part rainbow activity page (page 18) and fill in the rainbows and number pairs for 11, 12, 13 and 14.

CLASSROOM DRILL: Have the class give the number pairs for 13 and 14 in order. Write them on the board as described in Lesson Plan 1.

WORKSHEETS: Worksheets D and E are set up like A and B. (Note: refer to *Math Phonics™–Addition*, pages 84-85, for additional worksheets to practice these facts.) For an explanation of magic squares, see page 32 in *Math Phonics™–Decimals*.

OPTIONAL: Preview Lesson Plan 9 (pages 65-67)–A Gaggle of Great Ideas. Some of these games and activities could be used while you are teaching these earlier lesson plans.

Name _____

NUMBER PAIRS FOR _____

NUMBER PAIRS FOR _____

NUMBER PAIRS FOR _____

NUMBER PAIRS FOR _____

NUMBER PAIRS FOR 11

1 + 10
2 + 9
3 + 8
4 + 7
5 + 6

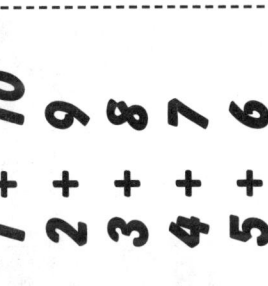

NUMBER PAIRS FOR 12

2 + 10
3 + 9
4 + 8
5 + 7
6 + 6

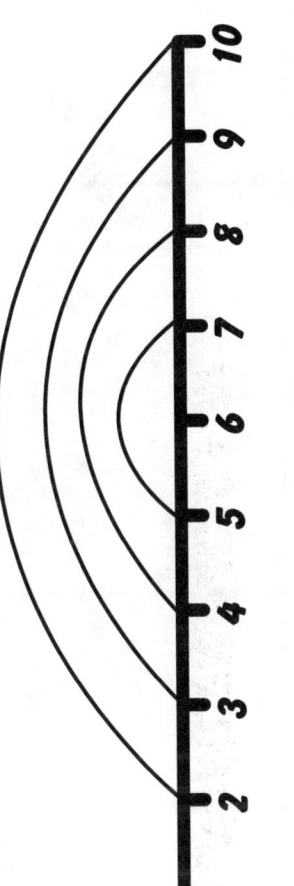

NUMBER PAIRS FOR 13

3 + 10
4 + 9
5 + 8
6 + 7

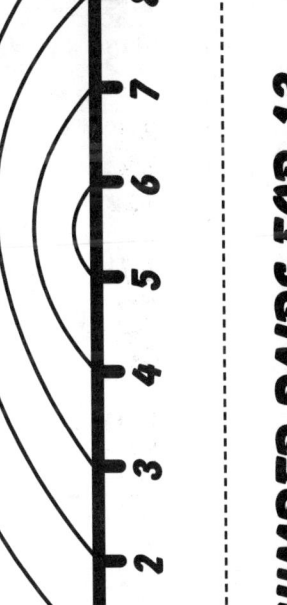

NUMBER PAIRS FOR 14

4 + 10
5 + 9
6 + 8
7 + 7

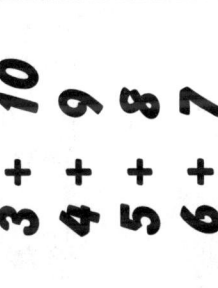
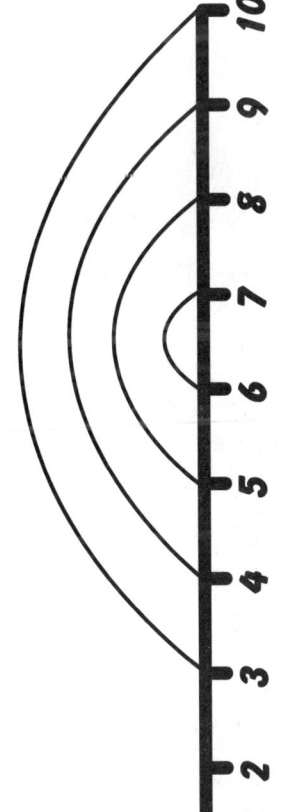
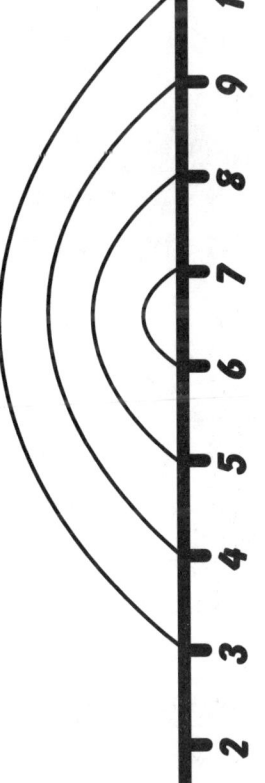

Name _____   **WORKSHEET D**

NUMBER PAIRS FOR 13 & 14

13	14
___ + 10	___ + 10
___ + ___	___ + 9
___ + ___	___ + 8
___ + ___	___ + 7

1. 10   9   8   7   6   5   4   3
   +3   +4   +5   +6   +7   +8   +9   +10

2. 10   9   8   7   6   5   4
   +4   +5   +6   +7   +8   +9   +10

Fill in the missing numbers. Use the problems above if you need help.

3. ☐   ☐   ☐   ☐   ☐   ☐   ☐   ☐
   +4   +9   +8   +5   +6   +7   +9   +4
   13   13   13   13   13   13   13   13

4. ☐   ☐   ☐   ☐   ☐   ☐   ☐   ☐
   +8   +6   +5   +9   +7   +5   +9   +7
   14   14   14   14   14   14   14   14

5. You have been told to order 8 packs of red paper and 6 packs of green paper before December 1st. How many total packs do you need to order? _____

6. There were 9 pieces of poster board used in Room A and 4 in Room B. How many were used in all? _____

CHALLENGE:
There has been a new math process discovered called the ☆ process. Here's how it works. 2☆ = 8 3☆ = 9 4☆ = 10 Find these answers: 6☆ = _____ 10☆ = _____. On the back of this paper tell how the ☆ process works.

Name _____   **WORKSHEET E**

MORE PRACTICE FOR 13s & 14s

Write out the number pairs for 13 and 14 if you need help.

1.   9   29   59   89   8   18   48   78
     +4   +4   +4   +4   +5   +5   +5   +5

2.   7   37   67   87   9   29   49   79
     +6   +6   +6   +6   +5   +5   +5   +5

3.   8   28   48   66   7   37   67   77
     +6   +6   +6   +8   +7   +7   +7   +7

REVIEW

4.   6   7   8   8   9   9   10   10
     +6   +4   +3   +4   +2   +3   +1   +2

5.   5   6   2   3   3   4   1   2
     +8   +8   +9   +9   +8   +8   +10   +10

6. Art class spent $14 on supplies and science class spent $9. What is the total of the two amounts? _____

7. Room A used 15 boxes of chalk and Room B used 6. What is the total number of boxes? _____

CHALLENGE:
Magic Square. Each row of three numbers (across, down or diagonal) has the same sum. What is the sum? _____ Fill in the missing numbers.

	1	8
	5	
	9	

TLC10345 Copyright © Teaching & Learning Company, Carthage, IL 62321-0010

Name _____   **WORKSHEET F**

MATH ART

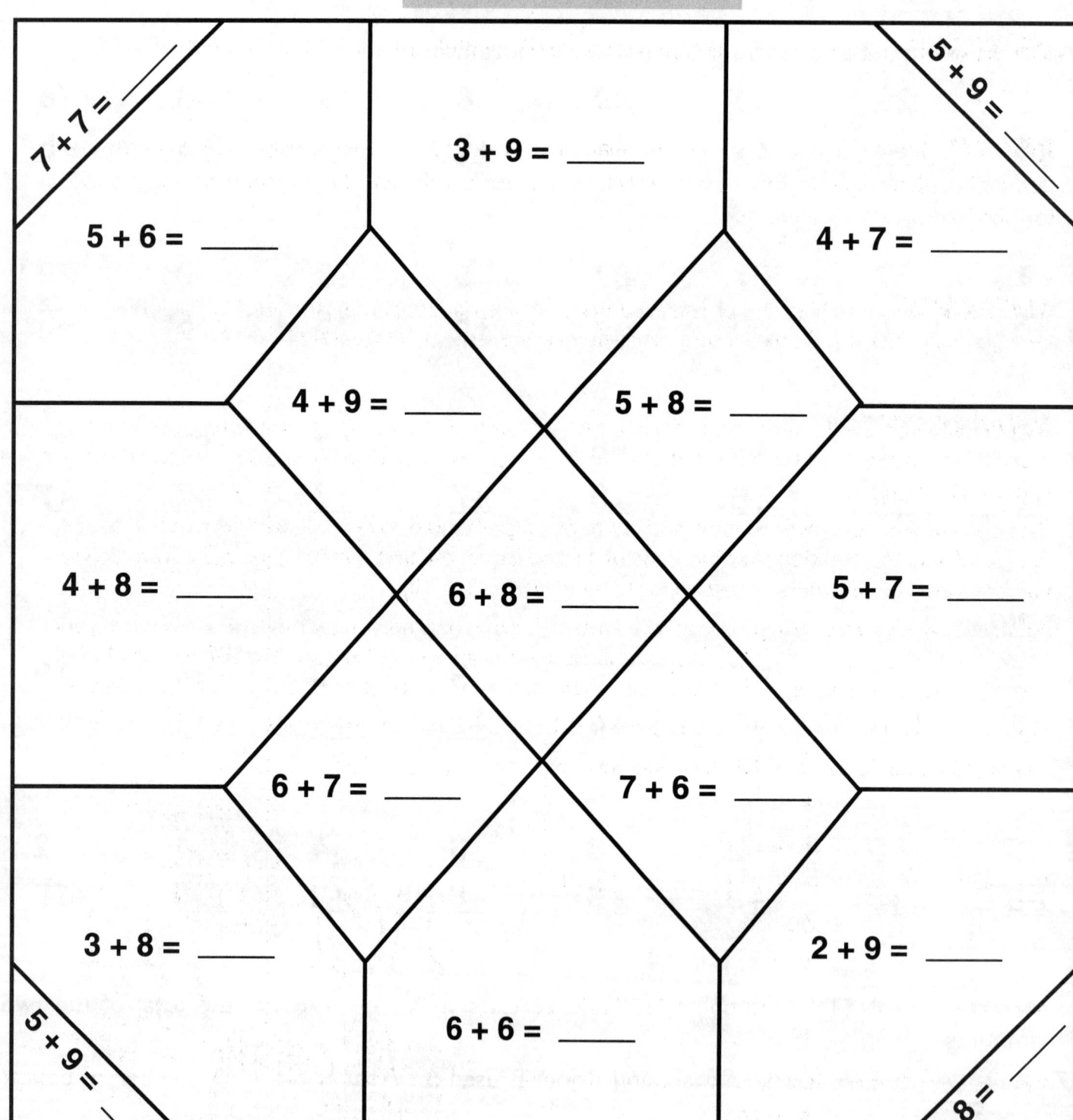

7 + 7 = ___
5 + 9 = ___
5 + 6 = ___
3 + 9 = ___
4 + 7 = ___
4 + 9 = ___
5 + 8 = ___
4 + 8 = ___
6 + 8 = ___
5 + 7 = ___
6 + 7 = ___
7 + 6 = ___
3 + 8 = ___
2 + 9 = ___
5 + 9 = ___
6 + 6 = ___
6 + 8 = ___

Choose four colors:

_____ if the answer is 11.   _____ if the answer is 12.

_____ if the answer is 13.   _____ if the answer is 14.

22

LESSON PLAN 3: ADDITION—15, 16, 17 & 18

OBJECTIVE: Give students addition practice with number pairs for 15, 16, 17 and 18.

REVIEW: Have students chant number pairs for 11, 12, 13 and 14 in unison. Continue this each day until students can say them easily. Have a volunteer check individual students to see if they can say number pairs for each group.

MATERIALS: movable number line (optional), ruler-sized number lines (page 11), "rainbow" activity page (page 18), 4 x 6 index cards or cardstock, worksheets (page 32-34)

DEMONSTRATION: Have students find number pairs for 15 using a movable number line if necessary. If all students understand moving fingers along the ruler, skip the movable number line and just use the ruler.

Pass out another four-way rainbow activity page (page 18) and have students find number pairs for 15, 16, 17 and 18. Mention that for sums of 11 and larger, the first number pair will always be some number plus 10. (Example: 15–the first number pair is 5 + 10)

If students seem to be "counting out" the answer for 5 + 10, review how the base 10 system works. They should see the 5 + 10 and automatically know the answer is 15. (See *Math Phonics™–Addition*, page 9, under the heading "Do" for an explanation of how to demonstrate the base 10 system.)

Point out how few number pairs there are for these last four groups of facts.

Besides the first fact of 5 + 10, they only need to learn two more facts for 15–

    6 + 9 = 15
    7 + 8 = 15

Besides 6 + 10, there are only two more facts for 16–

    7 + 9 = 16
    8 + 8 = 16

Besides 7 + 10, there is only one more fact for 17–

    8 + 9 = 17

Besides 8 + 10, there is only one more fact for 18–

    9 + 9 = 18

If they have learned doubles and number neighbors (*Math Phonics™–Addition*, lessons 4 and 5), 7 + 8, 8 + 8, 8 + 9 and 9 + 9 should be easy!

This makes the "big" numbers a lot less scary.

LESSON PLAN 3: CONTINUED

HANDOUT: Try this short version of the addition facts chart. (For longer version, see page 37 in *Math Phonics™–Addition*.)

Make copies of page 25 or page 26 on card stock or give each student a 4 x 6 index card. Students can divide their card into eight segments as shown on page 26. Students should refer to these mini facts charts for a day or two, and then return them to the teacher. Students should memorize the facts on these charts. They could be passed out later if students need a review.

CLASSROOM DRILL: Review number pairs for 11, 12, 13 and 14.

WORKSHEETS: Worksheets G and H, use directions for Worksheets A and B (page 10) in Lesson Plan 1.

T-Tables (pages 29-31) can be used as an in-class practice page, quiz or quick test (or Quest!).

OPTIONAL: If you have students who need help with sums less than 11, copy page 27 or page 28 for number pairs 7 through 18. Students could fill out another four-way rainbow activity page to find sums for 7, 8, 9 and 10. For sums of 10 and less, the first number pair is always 1 plus another number. Example:

$$1 + 6 = 7$$
$$2 + 5 = 7$$
$$3 + 4 = 7$$

The blank T-Table page could be used for subtraction practice in later lessons.

11s
1 + 10
2 + 9
3 + 8
4 + 7
5 + 6

12s
2 + 10
3 + 9
4 + 8
5 + 7
6 + 6

13s
3 + 10
4 + 9
5 + 8
6 + 7

14s
4 + 10
5 + 9
6 + 8
7 + 7

15s
5 + 10
6 + 9
7 + 8

16s
6 + 10
7 + 9
8 + 8

17s
7 + 10
8 + 9

18s
8 + 10
9 + 9

26

7s 1 + 6 2 + 5 3 + 4	**8s** 1 + 7 2 + 6 3 + 5 4 + 4	**9s** 1 + 8 2 + 7 3 + 6 4 + 5	**10s** 1 + 9 2 + 8 3 + 7 4 + 6 5 + 5	**11s** 1 + 10 2 + 9 3 + 8 4 + 7 5 + 6	**12s** 2 + 10 3 + 9 4 + 8 5 + 7 6 + 6
13s 3 + 10 4 + 9 5 + 8 6 + 7	**14s** 4 + 10 5 + 9 6 + 8 7 + 7	**15s** 5 + 10 6 + 9 7 + 8	**16s** 6 + 10 7 + 9 8 + 8	**17s** 7 + 10 8 + 9	**18s** 8 + 10 9 + 9

7s 1 + 6 2 + 5 3 + 4	**8s** 1 + 7 2 + 6 3 + 5 4 + 4	**9s** 1 + 8 2 + 7 3 + 6 4 + 5	**10s** 1 + 9 2 + 8 3 + 7 4 + 6 5 + 5	**11s** 1 + 10 2 + 9 3 + 8 4 + 7 5 + 6	**12s** 2 + 10 3 + 9 4 + 8 5 + 7 6 + 6
13s 3 + 10 4 + 9 5 + 8 6 + 7	**14s** 4 + 10 5 + 9 6 + 8 7 + 7	**15s** 5 + 10 6 + 9 7 + 8	**16s** 6 + 10 7 + 9 8 + 8	**17s** 7 + 10 8 + 9	**18s** 8 + 10 9 + 9

7s 1 + 6 2 + 5 3 + 4	**8s** 1 + 7 2 + 6 3 + 5 4 + 4	**9s** 1 + 8 2 + 7 3 + 6 4 + 5	**10s** 1 + 9 2 + 8 3 + 7 4 + 6 5 + 5	**11s** 1 + 10 2 + 9 3 + 8 4 + 7 5 + 6	**12s** 2 + 10 3 + 9 4 + 8 5 + 7 6 + 6
13s 3 + 10 4 + 9 5 + 8 6 + 7	**14s** 4 + 10 5 + 9 6 + 8 7 + 7	**15s** 5 + 10 6 + 9 7 + 8	**16s** 6 + 10 7 + 9 8 + 8	**17s** 7 + 10 8 + 9	**18s** 8 + 10 9 + 9

7s 1 + 6 2 + 5 3 + 4	**8s** 1 + 7 2 + 6 3 + 5 4 + 4	**9s** 1 + 8 2 + 7 3 + 6 4 + 5	**10s** 1 + 9 2 + 8 3 + 7 4 + 6 5 + 5	**11s** 1 + 10 2 + 9 3 + 8 4 + 7 5 + 6	**12s** 2 + 10 3 + 9 4 + 8 5 + 7 6 + 6
13s 3 + 10 4 + 9 5 + 8 6 + 7	**14s** 4 + 10 5 + 9 6 + 8 7 + 7	**15s** 5 + 10 6 + 9 7 + 8	**16s** 6 + 10 7 + 9 8 + 8	**17s** 7 + 10 8 + 9	**18s** 8 + 10 9 + 9

T-TABLES—ADDITION IN ORDER

	+2
2	
3	
4	
5	
6	
7	
8	
9	

	+3
2	
3	
4	
5	
6	
7	
8	
9	

	+4
2	
3	
4	
5	
6	
7	
8	
9	

	+5
2	
3	
4	
5	
6	
7	
8	
9	

	+6
2	
3	
4	
5	
6	
7	
8	
9	

	+7
2	
3	
4	
5	
6	
7	
8	
9	

	+8
2	
3	
4	
5	
6	
7	
8	
9	

	+9
2	
3	
4	
5	
6	
7	
8	
9	

	+10
2	
3	
4	
5	
6	
7	
8	
9	

T-TABLES—ADDITION NOT IN ORDER

	+2
3	
5	
7	
9	
2	
4	
6	
8	

	+3
4	
6	
8	
2	
9	
7	
5	
3	

	+4
6	
8	
2	
4	
7	
3	
9	
5	

	+5
9	
8	
2	
3	
7	
6	
4	
5	

	+6
2	
9	
3	
8	
4	
7	
5	
6	

	+7
3	
6	
9	
2	
5	
8	
4	
7	

	+8
7	
4	
2	
5	
8	
3	
6	
9	

	+9
3	
5	
8	
7	
5	
6	
9	
2	

	+10
5	
4	
9	
6	
3	
2	
7	
8	

Name _____

T-TABLES

Name _____ **WORKSHEET G**

NUMBER PAIRS FOR 15, 16, 17 & 18

Write the number pairs. Start with a number plus 10.

15	16	17	18
___ + 10	___ + 10	___ + 10	___ + 10
___ + ___	___ + ___	___ + ___	___ + ___
___ + ___	___ + ___		

1. 10   9   8   7   6   5   10   9   8
   +5 +6 +7 +8 +9 +10 +6 +7 +8

2. 7   6   10   9   8   7   10   9   8
   +9 +10 +7 +8 +9 +10 +8 +9 +10

Fill in the missing numbers. Use the problems above if you need help.

3. ☐   ☐   ☐   ☐   ☐   ☐
   +7   +8   +6   +9   +8   +7
   15   15   15   15   16   16

4. ☐   ☐   ☐   ☐   ☐   ☐
   +9   +8   +9   +9   +9   +6
   16   17   17   18   15   15

5. You see on the calendar that you will be on vacation 9 days and then home 7 days before school starts. How many days until school starts? _____

6. On the first day of vacation you hiked 8 miles and on the second day 7 miles. How many miles did you hike in all? _____

CHALLENGE:
I'm thinking of a number. When you double the number and add 6, the answer is 20. What is the number? _____

Name _____   **WORKSHEET H**

MORE PRACTICE FOR 15s, 16s, 17s & 18s

Write the number pairs if you need help.

1.   9   29   49   79   8   38   47   67
   +6   +16   +26   +16   +7   +17   +28   +18

2.   9   19   49   77   8   28   48   68
   +7   +37   +37   +19   +8   +38   +18   +28

3.   8   28   48   69   9   19   49   79
   +9   +39   +39   +28   +9   +29   +29   +19

REVIEW

4.   8   9   7   6   7   2   6   7
   +3   +5   +4   +6   +5   +9   +5   +7

5.   6   8   6   9   8   5   4   9
   +7   +4   +7   +5   +6   +8   +9   +3

5. You have spent $19 on rides and $18 on games. How much in all? _____

6. After driving 8 hours yesterday, your family drove 13 hours today. How many hours in all? _____

CHALLENGE:
What is the largest four-digit number that can be made using all the same digit? _____ Using four different digits? _____

Name _____   WORKSHEET 1

MATH MAZE

Write in all the answers. Then find a path from Start to Finish going through circles that have the same answer. If you hit a dead end, backtrack and try another way.

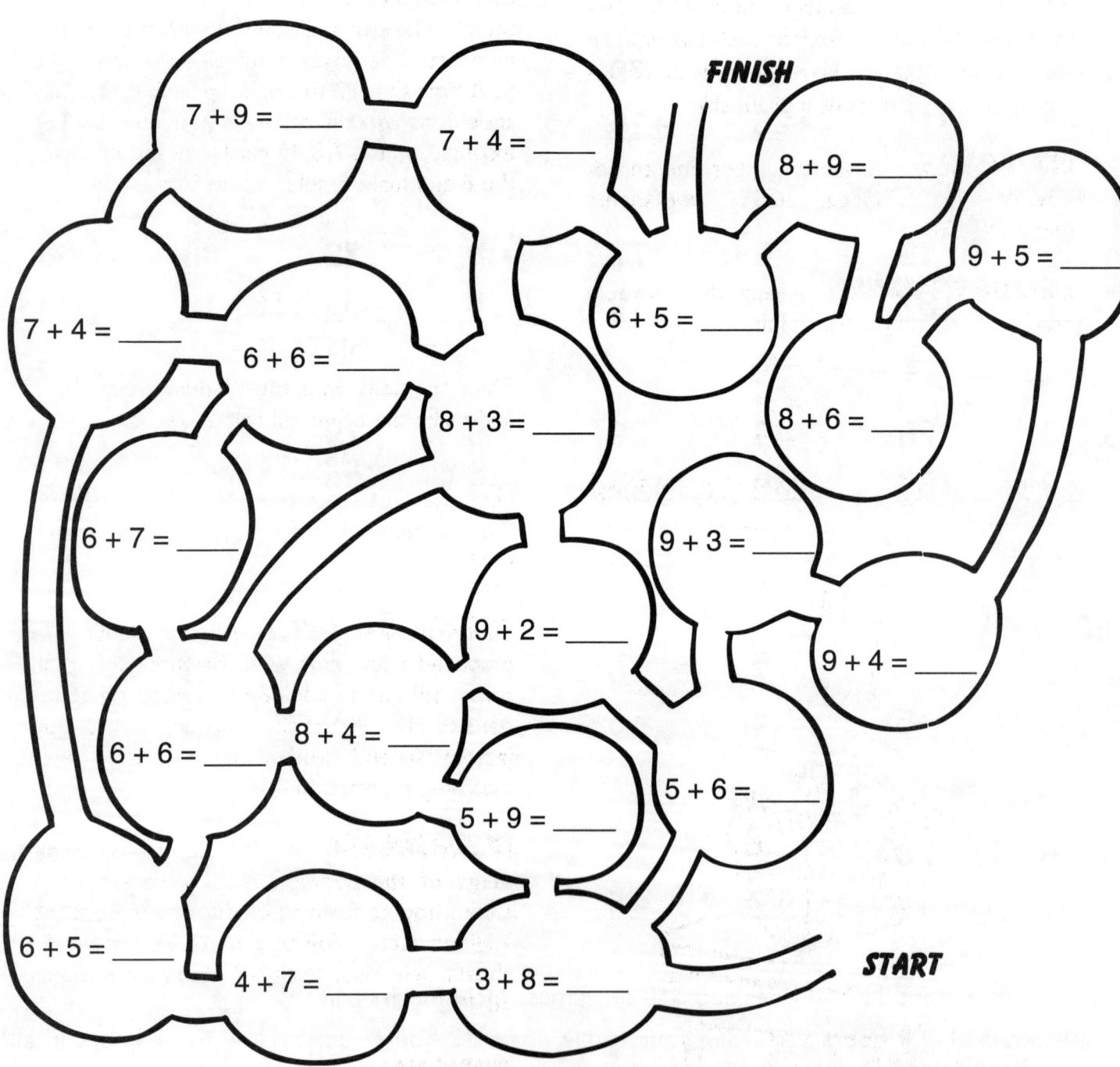

34   TLC10345 Copyright © Teaching & Learning Company, Carthage, IL 62321-0010

LESSON PLAN 4: THREE-WAY FLASH CARDS

OBJECTIVE: Show students how to form subtraction problems from the addition facts they have learned using three-way flash cards.

REVIEW: Have students chant number pairs for 15, 16, 17 and 18. Repeat each day until all students know them. Have a parent or volunteer check each student individually.

MATERIALS: movable number line, three-way flash cards (pages 36-39), worksheets (pages 40-42)

DEMONSTRATION: Using the movable number line, demonstrate that

$$6 + 7 = 13$$
$$13 - 7 = 6$$
$$13 - 6 = 7$$

13

Use other examples as needed.

HANDOUT: Give each student a set of three-way flash cards. Have students cut them apart. The backs should be blank. When students go through the flash cards the first time, they should cover the lower number with one thumb. Make an addition fact with the two top numbers. The lower number is the sum. The next time they go through the flash cards, they should cover one of the top numbers. For example, on the 7, 8, 15 card they should cover the 8 and make a subtraction fact:

$$15 - 7 = 8$$

Then, the next time, they should cover the 7 and make the other subtraction fact:

$$15 - 8 = 7$$

Have students write the one addition fact and the two subtraction facts on the back of each card.

CLASSROOM DRILL: After students have practiced a few days with the three-way flash cards, call out an addition fact. Call on a student to give one of the matching subtraction facts—a second student to give the other matching subtraction fact.

WORKSHEETS: Worksheet J reminds students of the addition facts. Worksheet K shows how to form subtraction facts from the addition facts. For two more similar worksheets, see *Math Phonics™—Subtraction*, pages 18-19.

OPTIONAL: After students have completed the crossword puzzle on Worksheet L, give a spelling test using the 10 number words on the puzzle.

4	7	3
2 6	2 9	3 6
3	6	9
2 5	2 8	2 11
2	5	8
2 4	2 7	2 10

6 · 3 = 9	9 · 3 = 12	6 · 4 = 10
5 · 3 = 8	8 · 3 = 11	5 · 4 = 9
4 · 3 = 7	7 · 3 = 10	4 · 4 = 8

37

9 / 13 / 4	7 / 12 / 5	6 / 12 / 6
8 / 12 / 4	6 / 11 / 5	9 / 14 / 5
7 / 11 / 4	5 / 10 / 5	8 / 13 / 5

6 9 15	7 9 16	9 9 18
6 8 14	7 8 15	8 9 17
6 7 13	7 7 14	8 8 16

Name _____   **WORKSHEET J**

REVIEW–ADDITION FACTS–SUMS 11-18

1. 4   6   7   4   8   10   4
   +7   +9   +7   +8   +9   +7   +9

2. 7   10   6   9   10   7   10
   +9   +8   +6   +2   +2   +8   +6

3. 6   9   5   6   10   3   10
   +7   +3   +10   +8   +3   +8   +1

4. 5   5   8   10   7   9   8
   +6   +9   +8   +4   +5   +9   +5

SUMS OF 4-10 (NO ZEROS OR ONES)

5. 5   6   3   2   4   6   8   4
   +5   +2   +2   +4   +4   +3   +2   +3

6. 2   5   3   6   7   3   7   5
   +2   +2   +5   +4   +2   +3   +3   +4

LARGER NUMBERS

7. 24   38   54   27   66   78   49   52
   +7   +9   +8   +9   +8   +7   +2   +8

8. 33   52   18   29   68   37   49   67
  +66   +47   +34   +49   +28   +47   +23   +26

9. 27   67   57   46   66   24   47   36
  +54   +13   +25   +29   +25   +36   +29   +46

Name _____   **WORKSHEET K**

NUMBER PAIRS—SUBTRACTION PRACTICE

For each addition problem, form two subtraction problems.

1. 8   13   13   7   ☐   ☐   9   ☐   ☐
   +5 -8   -5   +4 -7 -4 +3 -9 -3
   13   5   8   ☐   ☐

2. 9   ☐   ☐   6   ☐   ☐   7   ☐   ☐
   +5 -9 -5 +7 -6 -7 +8 -7 -8
   ☐   ☐

3. 7   ☐   ☐   8   ☐   ☐   6   ☐   ☐
   +9 -7 -9 +3 -8 -3 +8 -6 -8
   ☐   ☐   ☐

4. 4   ☐   ☐   5   ☐   ☐   9   ☐   ☐
   +9 -9 -4 +6 -6 -5 +8 -9 -8
   ☐   ☐   ☐

For each addition doubles problem, there is only one subtraction problem.

5. 5   ☐   6   ☐   7   ☐   8   ☐   9   ☐
   +5 -5 +6 -6 +7 -7 +8 -8 +9 -9
   ☐   ☐   ☐   ☐   ☐

5. When you arrived at the amusement park, you had $16. At noon, you had $7 left. How much money did you spend? _____

6. There are 15 rides. You have ridden 8. How many rides are left? _____

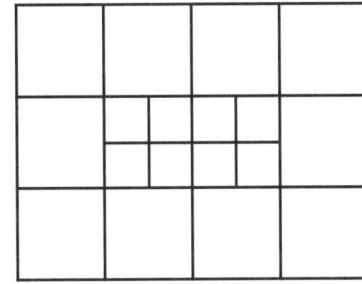

CHALLENGE:
How many squares are contained in this figure? _____

41

TLC10345 Copyright © Teaching & Learning Company, Carthage, IL 62321-0010

CROSSWORD PUZZLE

WORKSHEET L

Use these words:

**eleven
twelve
thirteen
fourteen
fifteen
sixteen
seventeen
eighteen
nineteen
twenty**

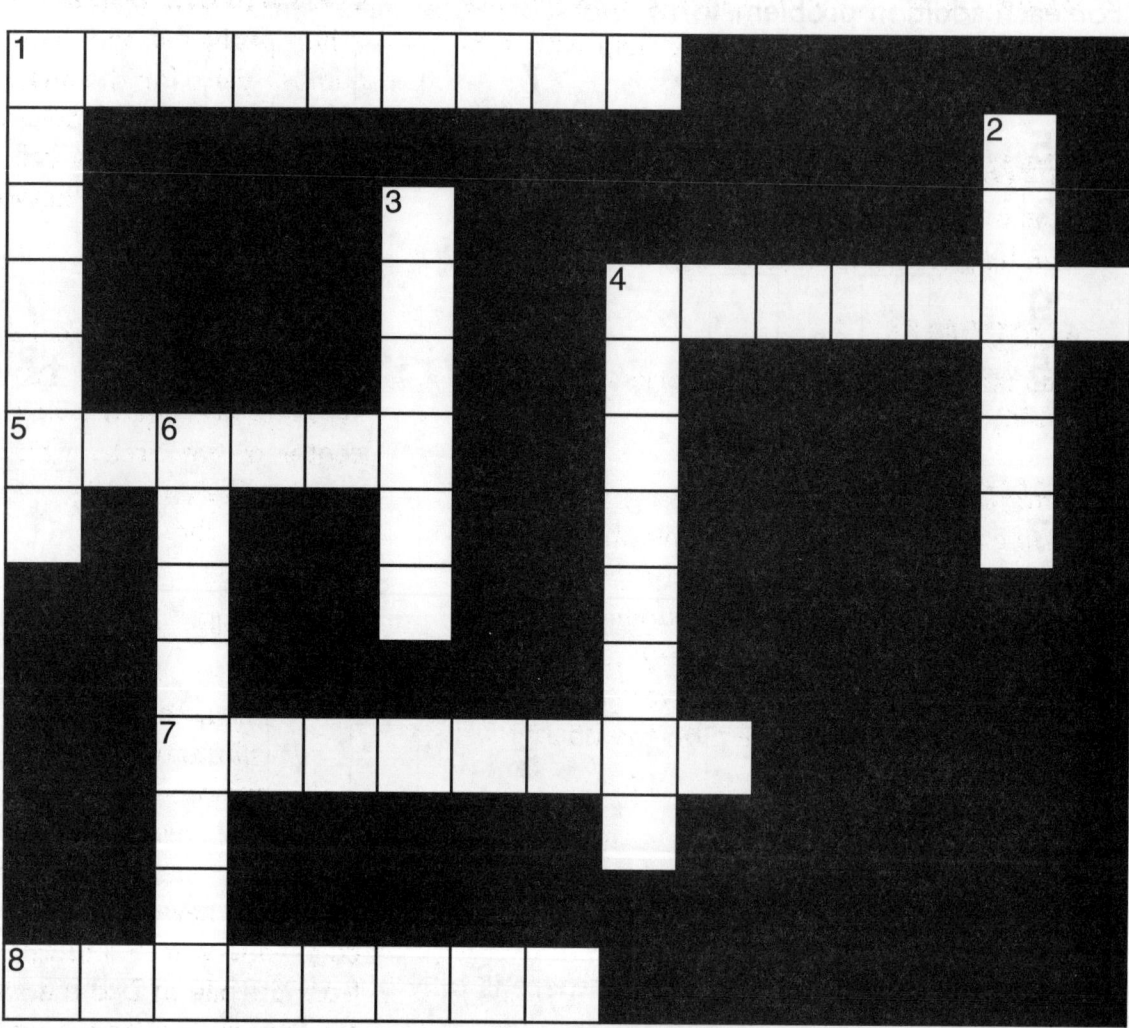

ACROSS

1. 9 + 8 = _____
4. 5 + 10 = _____
5. 8 + 3 = _____
7. 6 + 7 = _____
8. 9 + 10 = _____

DOWN

1. 8 + 8 = _____
2. 9 + 3 = _____
3. 10 + 10 = _____
4. 7 + 7 = _____
6. 9 + 9 = _____

LESSON PLAN 5: SUBTRACTION—11 & 12 AS MINUENDS

OBJECTIVE: Show students how to use number pairs for 11 and 12 to help with subtraction.

REVIEW: Write two or three addition problems on the board and ask students to give the matching subtraction problems for each.

MATERIALS: mini facts charts (page 27), worksheets (pages 44-46)

DEMONSTRATION: By this time students should be able to call to mind number pairs for 11 and 12 without number lines, students at the front of the room and rainbows. However, you may use those if necessary to begin the discussion. Ask students to give number pairs for 11 and 12. Write them on the board.

11	12
1 + 10	2 + 10
2 + 9	3 + 9
3 + 8	4 + 8
4 + 7	5 + 7
5 + 6	6 + 6

Now if students had a problem with 11 - 8 and could not think of the answer, they could look at the number pairs for 11 on the mini facts chart. Go down until they find the 8. Since 8 + 3 = 11, 11 - 8 = 3.

✪✪✪✪✪✪✪✪ + ✪✪✪

11

You may need to explain this several times before all students grasp it.

CLASSROOM DRILL: Give students some other problems and have them look at the number pairs for the answer. Read the problems in rows 1 and 2 of Worksheet N one at a time. Have the class call out answers. Mix them up and ask for answers from individual students.

WORKSHEETS: Worksheets M and N are self-explanatory. For Worksheet O, be sure students are not drawing a line through the center of the circle. This would give a completely different design. Refer to the answer key to see the design.

OPTIONAL: Teach the three subtraction terms:

    minuend   11
    subtractor - 8
    difference   3

The word *minuend* always refers to the top number in subtraction. On Worksheet N, Challenge, have students think of two piles of coins—one with 9 and one with 2. Move one from the pile of 2 to the pile of 9 making 10 in the larger pile and 1 in the other. Now, 10 + 1 = 11.

Name _____ **WORKSHEET M**

11 & 12 AS MINUENDS

Write the addition number pairs for 11 and 12.

11	12
1 + 10	2 + 10
___ + ___	___ + ___
___ + ___	___ + ___
___ + ___	___ + ___
___ + ___	___ + ___

Fold on the dotted line. If you can't think of a subtraction answer look up a number pair to help.

Example: 12   Look at number pairs for 12.
          - 5   Since 5 + 7 = 12, 12 - 5 = 7.

↦↦↦↦↦ ↦↦↦↦↦↦↦
         12

----

1. 12   11   12   11   12   11   12   11
    -5   -3   -6   -4   -7   -5   -8   -6

2. 12   11   12   11   12   11   11
    -9   -7   -3   -8   -4   -9   -2

3. The temperature yesterday was 12°F. Today it is 5°F. How much did the temperature drop? _____

4. Average rainfall for your town is 11 inches. This year you have received 7 inches. How many inches below average is that? _____

CHALLENGE:
Find the missing numbers in this addition problem:
```
  133
  525
 +21☐
 ☐71
```

44

Name _____   **WORKSHEET N**

11 & 12 AS MINUENDS

Write the answers to these subtraction problems. Then make a "rainbow" connecting matching facts–two problems which have the same three numbers.

1. 11   11   11   11   11   11   11   11
    -2   -3   -4   -5   -6   -7   -8   -9
    ――― ――― ――― ――― ――― ――― ――― ―――
     9   2

2. 12   12   12   12   12   12   12
    -3   -4   -5   -6   -7   -8   -9
    ――― ――― ――― ――― ――― ――― ―――

REVIEW: SUMS FOR 11 & 12

3.   5   8   6   8   5   9   2   4
    +7   +3   +6   +4   +6   +3   +9   +7
    ――― ――― ――― ――― ――― ――― ――― ―――

REVIEW: SUMS FOR 13 & 14

4.   9   6   9   5   7   6
    +4   +7   +5   +8   +7   +8
    ――― ――― ――― ――― ――― ―――

5. It is 12 minutes until school ends. You work another 8 minutes on your homework. Now how much time is left? _____

6. It was 11°F outside when you got home from school. One hour later it was 8°F. How much did the temperature drop? _____

CHALLENGE:
Do these problems and then fill in the blank. When you add 9 to a number, the answer in the ones place is _____ less than the top number.

   2   3   4   5   6   7   8   9
  +9   +9   +9   +9   +9   +9   +9   +9
  ――― ――― ――― ――― ――― ――― ――― ―――

45

Name _____

WORKSHEET O

MATH WEAVE

Write in all the correct answers. Then connect each dot to the next dot with the same answer going clockwise around the circle.

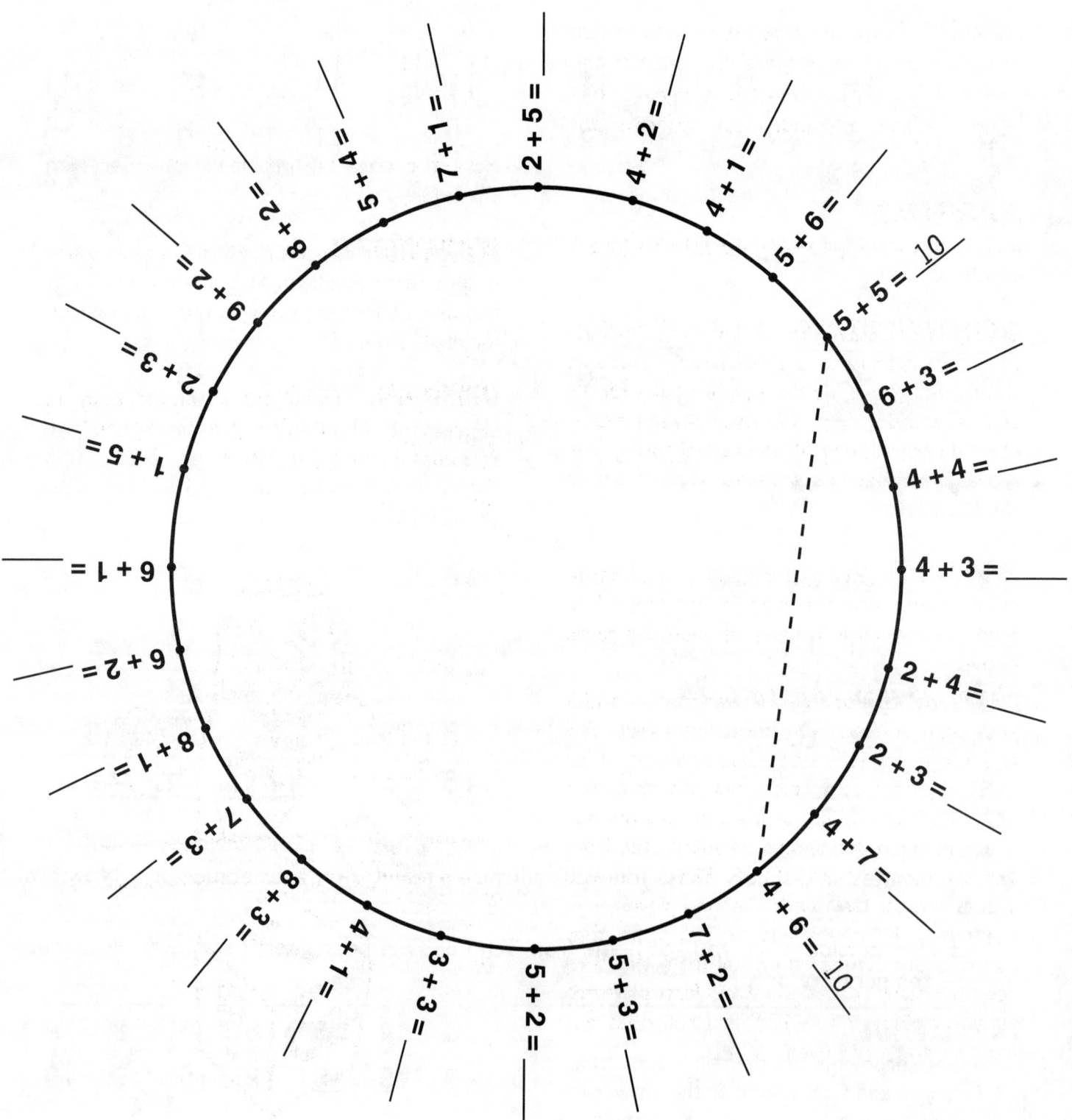

46

LESSON PLAN 6: SUBTRACTION—13 & 14 AS MINUENDS

OBJECTIVE: Show students how to use addition number pairs for 13 and 14 to find answers to subtraction.

REVIEW: Read the problem in the top two rows of Worksheet N (page 45) in order and have the class say the answers as a group. Mix them up and ask individual students for answers.

MATERIALS: mini facts charts (page 27), worksheets (pages 48-49)

DEMONSTRATION: Follow the instructions for Lesson Plan 5 if necessary. Students should be able to list the number pairs for 13 and 14 without help. Go over several examples, demonstrating if necessary using the movable number line, students at the front of the room, etc.

HANDOUT: Give each student a copy of the game, Subtraction Stepping-Stones (page 50). Students may play in pairs or take the game home.

Directions: Use one die. Cover the 1, 2 and 3 with blank stickers. On the stickers write 7, 8 and 9, one on each side. Use coins or other small objects for movers. First player moves onto the first stepping-stone and rolls the die. The number rolled should be subtracted from 14. If you roll a 6, 14 - 6 = 8. Player moves 8 spaces and the turn ends. Second player does the same. If players land on roll again, they subtract the number they roll from the 10 to see how many spaces to move. First player to arrive at Finish wins. The final roll does not need to come out even.

CLASSROOM DRILL: Write these problems on the board without answers:

13	13	13	13	13	13
-9	-8	-7	-6	-5	-4

14	14	14	14	14
-9	-8	-7	-6	-5

Have the class say problems in order with answers.

WORKSHEETS: Worksheet Q has a review of all subtraction facts with 11 through 14 as minuend. These are some of the most difficult for most students.

OPTIONAL: Hand out a second copy of Worksheets M, N and P if necessary to give students more practice. See *Math Phonics™—Subtraction*, pages 84-85 for additional practice.

Name _____   **WORKSHEET P**

13 & 14 AS MINUENDS

Write the addition number pairs for 13 and 14.

13	14
___ + 10	___ + 10
___ + ___	___ + ___
___ + ___	___ + ___
___ + ___	___ + ___

Use the number pairs to help you with these subtraction problems, if you need help.

1. 13   14   13   14   13   14
   -9   -5   -8   -6   -7   -7

2. 13   14   13   14   13
   -6   -8   -5   -9   -4

REVIEW

3. 11   12   11   12   11   12   11   12
   -6   -8   -5   -7   -4   -6   -3   -5

4. 12   11   12   11   12   11   11
   -9   -7   -3   -8   -4   -9   -2

5. The music teacher has said you need to practice 14 hours before the band contest. If you have already practiced 9 hours, how many more do you need to practice? _____

6. Your teacher has given you 13 pages of sheet music. If you can find 8 sheets, how many have you lost? _____

CHALLENGE:
What is the smallest number you can write using four different digits (not including zero)? _____

Name _____   **WORKSHEET Q**

PRACTICE! 11-14 AS MINUENDS

1. 12   11   13   14   11   12   11
    -3   -6   -9   -8   -4   -9   -2

2. 13   14   11   12   14   13
    -4   -9   -8   -4   -5   -8

3. 11   12   13   14   12   11   13
    -7   -8   -7   -7   -6   -3   -5

4. 11   12   14   11   13   12
    -9   -7   -6   -5   -6   -5

REVIEW

5. 9   8   7   9   8   9   6   7
    +6   +8   +9   +8   +7   +9   +8   +9

6. 14 students have entered the science fair. 9 are girls. How many boys are entered? _____

7. 12 students got As or Bs. If 8 got a B, how many got an A? _____

CHALLENGE:
I'm thinking of a number. The numeral in the hundreds place is twice as large as the numeral in the ones place. There is a 0 in the tens place. There is a 6 in the hundreds place. What is the number? _____

SUBTRACTION STEPPING-STONES

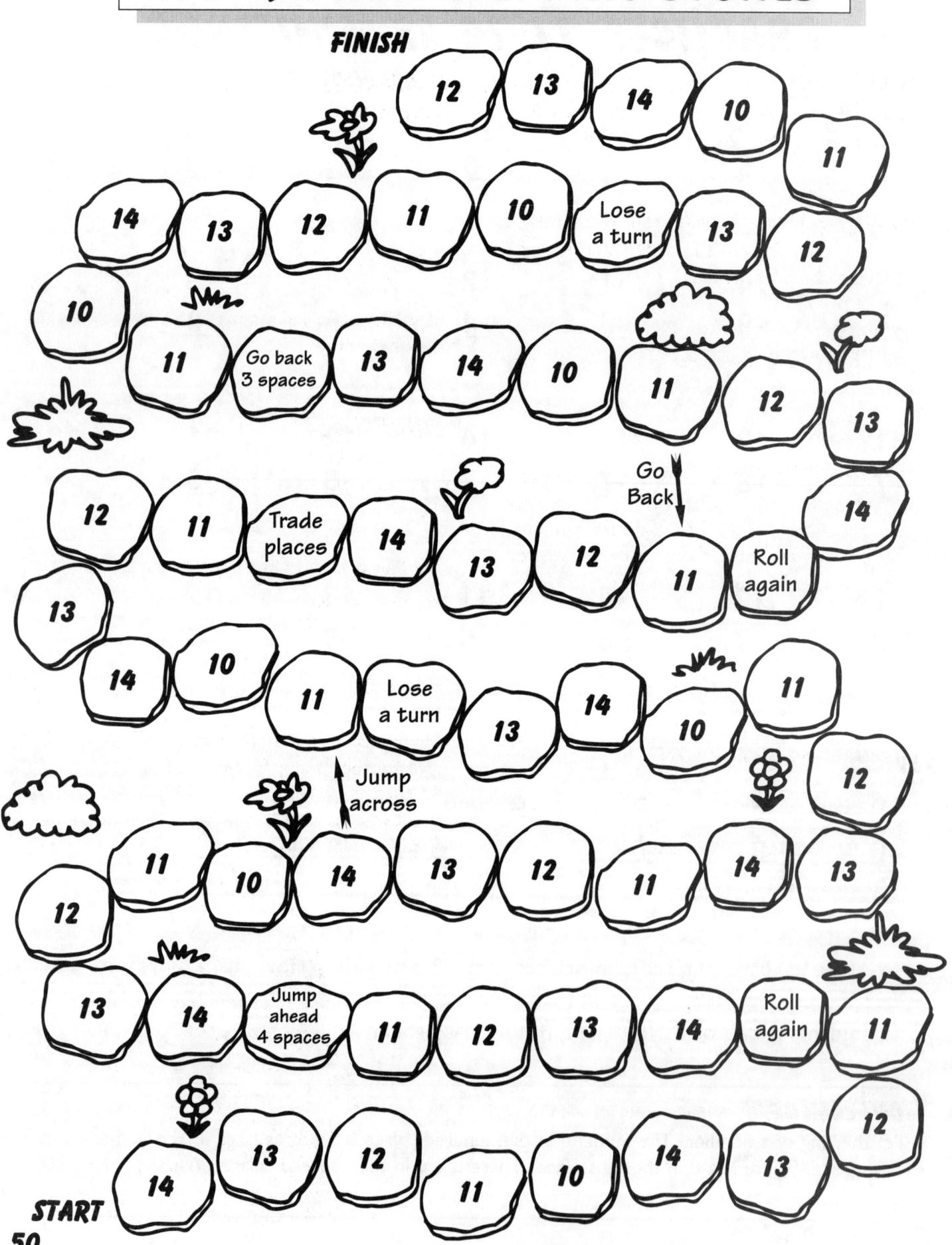

LESSON PLAN 7: SUBTRACTION—15, 16, 17 & 18 AS MINUENDS

OBJECTIVE: Show students how to use number pairs for 15, 16, 17 and 18 to find answers to subtraction problems.

REVIEW: Have the class chant the subtraction facts for 13 and 14 in order. Write them on the board if necessary.

MATERIALS: mini facts charts (page 27), worksheets (pages 52-55)

DEMONSTRATION: Follow instructions from Lesson Plan 5. Go through all subtraction problems for 15-18. Be sure students notice how few facts there are to learn for these groups. There is only one for 18:

$$18 - 9 = 9$$

There are only two for 17:

$$17 - 8 = 9$$
$$17 - 9 = 8$$

There are only three for 16:

$$16 - 8 = 8$$
$$16 - 9 = 7$$
$$16 - 7 = 9$$

There are only four for 15:

$$15 - 6 = 9$$
$$15 - 7 = 8$$
$$15 - 8 = 7$$
$$15 - 9 = 6$$

HANDOUT: Worksheet T can be used as a regular worksheet or as a race between two people or two teams.

CLASSROOM DRILL: Write these problems on the board:

```
 15    15    15    15    16    16    16
 -9    -8    -7    -6    -9    -8    -7

 17    17    18
 -9    -8    -9
```

Have the class say the problems in order with the answers.

WORKSHEETS: Notice that in rows 3 and 4 of Worksheet R there will be several problems with the same answer in the ones place.

OPTIONAL: TWO MEMORY TRICKS

Pay with the Dime: For 11 - 9, think of having a dime and a penny and spending 9¢. Pay with the dime and get a penny back to put with your other penny. 11 - 9 = 2

Bingo 9: For 16 - 7, think of having a dime and 6 pennies. You give the 6 pennies and have to give another penny from the dime. That leaves 9¢ change from the dime. 16 - 7 = 9 When the lower number is one more than the upper number, think Bingo 9.

Name _____   **WORKSHEET R**

15, 16, 17 & 18 AS MINUENDS

Write the addition number pairs for 15, 16, 17 and 18.

15	16	17	18
___ + 10	___ + 10	___ + 10	___ + 10
___ + ___	___ + ___	___ + ___	___ + ___
___ + ___	___ + ___		

Use these number pairs if you need help with these problems:

1. 15   17   16   18   16
    -6   -9   -9   -9   -8

2. 15   15   16   17   15
    -9   -8   -7   -8   -7

REVIEW

3. 36   46   26   58   38   27   48
    +9   +29   +49   +8   +28   +8   +27

4. 37   47   77   29   49   39   69
   +19   +29   +19   +28   +18   +29   +29

5. Your rocket flew 17 feet. Your friend's rocket flew 9 feet. How much farther did yours fly? _____

6. You spent $18 on your rocket. Your friend spent $9. How much more did you spend? _____

CHALLENGE:
Gene, Joan, Jan and John won the top 4 ribbons in the science fair. Joan took second and Jan did not take 4th. If Gene took 3rd, which ribbon did John win? _____

52   TLC10345 Copyright © Teaching & Learning Company, Carthage, IL 62321-0010

Name _____   **WORKSHEET 5**

15, 16, 17 & 18 AS MINUENDS

1. 17   15   18   16   17   15   16
    -9   -7   -9   -9   -8   -8   -8

2. 15   16   15   16   17   18   15
    -6   -7   -9   -8   -9   -9   -8

ADDITION REVIEW

3. 137   238   369   128   526   617   356
    +259   +428   +228   +358   +349   +278   +219

4. 278   165   318   409   549   218   139
    +319   +429   +267   +326   +137   +348   +406

5. 207   348   606   345   267   139   136
    +386   +125   +136   +137   +127   +204   +248

6. The art class spent $16 on supplies; $9 of it was for paint. The rest was for art paper. How much was spent for paper? _____

7. Parents donated $15 for prizes; $8 of it was for trophies. The rest was for ribbons. How much did the ribbons cost? _____

CHALLENGE:
Do these subtraction problems and then fill in the blank.

11   12   13   14   15   16   17   18
-9   -9   -9   -9   -9   -9   -9   -9

When you subtract 9 from a number, the number in the ones place of the answer is _____ _____ than the number in the ones place of the minuend.

53

Name _____ WORKSHEET T

BRAIN-POWERED ELEVATOR!

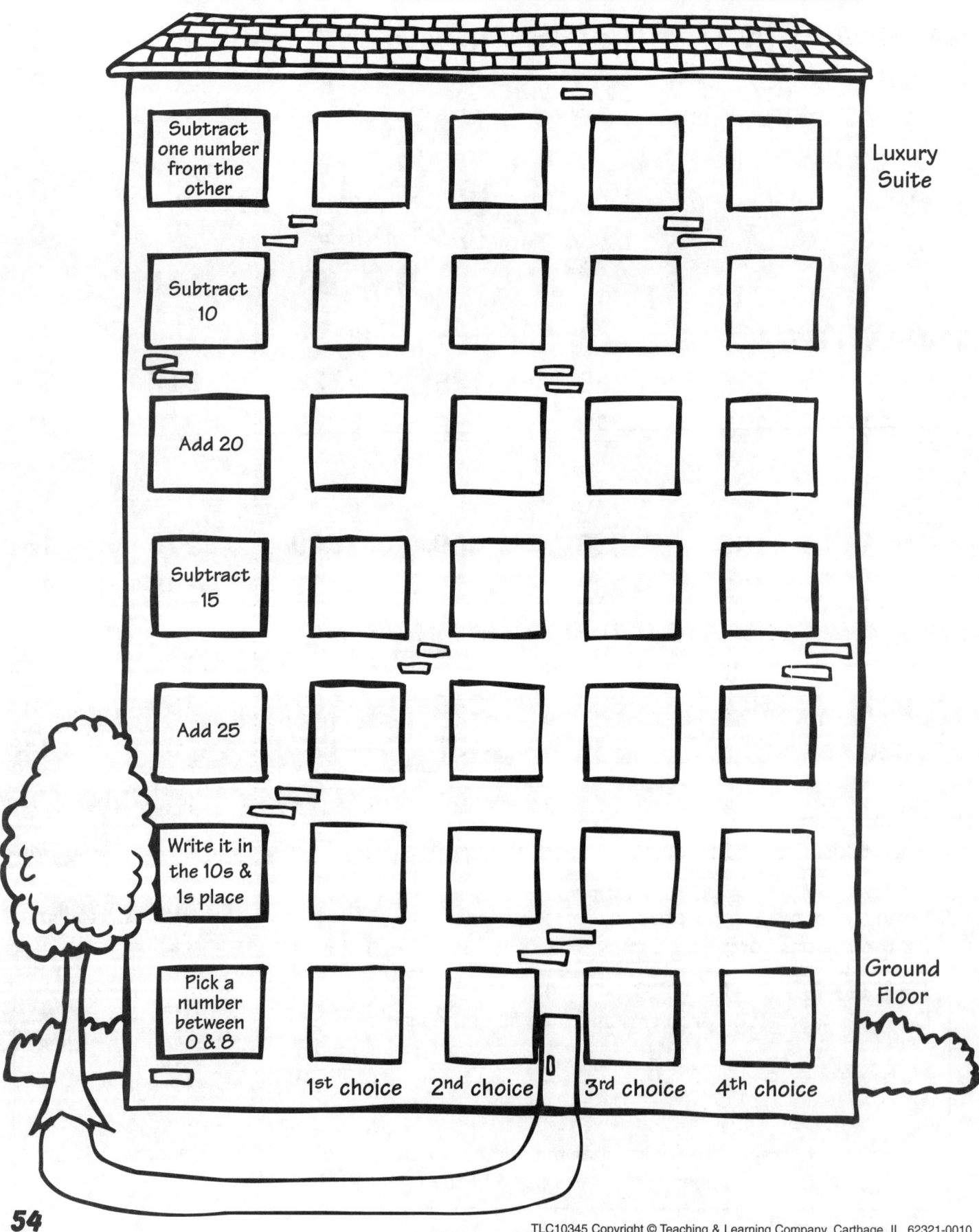

Name _____   **WORKSHEET U**

REVIEW

SUBTRACTION WITH 11-18 AS MINUEND

1. 13   11   15   18   12   14   16   17   11
   -7   -9   -6   -9   -6   -5   -9   -8   -2

2. 12   11   13   15   14   17   12   11   16
   -3   -8   -9   -7   -7   -9   -4   -3   -8

3. 11   15   16   13   11   12   14   13   12
   -4   -8   -7   -4   -5   -9   -9   -5   -5

4. 11   13   15   14   12   11   14   13   12
   -7   -8   -9   -6   -8   -6   -8   -6   -7

SUBTRACTION WITH 2-10 AS MINUEND (NO ZEROS)

5. 7   10   6   3   5   10   8   4   10   7   8
   -1   -9   -2   -1 -3   -5   -4 -2 -2   -6   -5

6. 9   10   8   7   2   9   7   6   8   10   9
   -3   -7   -1 -2 -1 -4 -3 -1 -2   -6   -8

7. 7   4   10   8   5   6   9   10   9   7   8
   -4 -3   -8 -3 -4 -3 -7 -4 -1 -5   -7

8. 3   5   10   9   9   4   6   8   5   6   9
   -2 -1   -3 -5 -6 -1 -5 -6 -2 -4   -2

55

LESSON PLAN 8: REGROUPING IN SUBTRACTION

OBJECTIVE: Demonstrate and teach the concept of regrouping (borrowing) using play money.

DEMONSTRATION: Divide students into groups of two. Give each group 20 of the play one dollar bills and eight of the play $10 bills. Tell them they are going to make change. Here is the problem. They have $36. Have each one count out six ones and three of the 10s. The other money should be placed in a separate pile. They are purchasing an item costing $9. They need to change one of the $10 bills to 10 ones. This is what happens when they regroup for subtraction.

    3 tens   6 ones   becomes

    2 tens   16 ones

Now they can pay the $9. 16 - 9 = 7. They should count this out. What do they have left? This is how the problem looks for subtraction:

```
                        2 16
    36    regrouping    3̶6̶
    -9                  -9
                        27
```

Other examples:

You have 45 comic books. You are giving away 8. How many are left?

You have 63 music CDs. You are loaning your friend 9 of them. How many do you have left?

Use Worksheets V and W (pages 60-61) for practice. Then teach regrouping using the hundred dollar bills, also. Pass out three of the $100 bills.

Examples:

You have $235. You are spending $45 for a new radio. How much change will you get back?

```
                         1 13
    235    regrouping    2̶3̶5
    -45                  -45
                         190
```

You have $308. You are spending $83. How much will you have left?

```
                         2 10
    308    regrouping    3̶0̶8
    -83                  -83
                         225
```

Use Worksheets X and Y (pages 62-63) to practice this. For these two worksheets there will be regrouping from 100 to 10s only.

56   TLC10345 Copyright © Teaching & Learning Company, Carthage, IL 62321-0010

WORKSHEET V

Name _____

REGROUP & SUBTRACT

1. 45   55   65   76   86   96   43   53   63
  -17 -17 -17 -29 -29 -29 -16 -16 -16

2. 38   58   78   67   77   87   24   44   64
  -19 -19 -19 -29 -29 -29 -19 -19 -19

3. 42   62   82   51   61   71   35   45   55
  -17 -17 -17 -14 -14 -14 -18 -18 -18

4. 41   51   61   36   56   76   33   43   53
  -18 -18 -18 -18 -18 -18 -15 -15 -15

5. 37   47   57   46   66   86   55   65   75
  -18 -18 -18 -27 -27 -27 -36 -36 -36

6. 34   44   54   45   55   65   33   43   53
  -17 -17 -17 -29 -29 -29 -19 -19 -19

7. A total of 85 people came to the science fair. If 49 came on Friday how many came on Saturday? _____

8. The school took in $98 at the science fair and had $59 in expenses. How much money did the school get to keep? _____

CHALLENGE:
If you earn $2 on Monday, double that much on Tuesday, double Tuesday's amount on Wednesday and continue doubling each day, how much will you earn the following Sunday? What is your total amount earned for all seven days? _____

Name _____ **WORKSHEET W**

REGROUP & SUBTRACT

1. 75   86   93   38   62   52   92
   -38   -27   -29   -19   -18   -37   -36

2. 67   91   88   70   57   33   46
   -38   -17   -69   -18   -29   -16   -28

3. 44   56   63   72   83   75   66
   -17   -18   -29   -28   -17   -26   -19

4. 63   75   53   45   51   50   64
   -28   -47   -29   -29   -18   -23   -27

5. 58   41   33   65   78   81   92
   -29   -26   -28   -39   -49   -54   -36

6. 87   94   87   61   54   42   57
   -48   -46   -38   -39   -28   -15   -29

7. Your class has collected 93 pounds of food for the homeless shelter. The class next door collected 75 pounds. How many more pounds did your class collect? _____

8. You counted 53 cans of fruit and 26 cans of vegetables. How many more cans of fruit are there? _____

CHALLENGE:
Try this number puzzle three times and then try it on a friend or parent. Announce that you can tell them ahead of time what their answer will be!
Puzzle: First number—choose any one-digit number.
  Second number—put your first number in the 10s place followed by a 0.
  Third number—subtract—second number minus the first number.
  Fourth number—add 9 to the last answer.
  Now add the two numerals of the fourth number.
  The answer is always 9!

Name _____   **WORKSHEET X**

REGROUP & SUBTRACT

1. 135   239   337   146   248   343
    -64   -48   -56   -72   -64   -81

2. 122   225   328   153   259   356
    -61   -63   -64   -72   -78   -74

3. 163   268   364   175   271   374
    -71   -86   -83   -92   -81   -80

4. 214   319   416   187   281   387
    -73   -62   -53   -94   -90   -94

5. 247   345   448   139   234   438
    -53   -51   -93   -72   -83   -95

Subtract. Then put each letter in its matching blank to solve the puzzle.

Puzzle: How do you spell an eight-letter word with one letter? _____

6. 236   347   456   269   128   315
    -45   -74   -92   -93   -76   -72

    P   E   O   L   V   N

    ___   ___   ___   ___   ___   ___   ___   ___
    273   243   52   273   176   364   191   273

62

TLC10345 Copyright © Teaching & Learning Company, Carthage, IL 62321-0010

Name _____   **WORKSHEET Y**

REGROUP & SUBTRACT

1. 285   126   259   327   428   234
   -36   -19   -68   -46   -87   -53

2. 523   486   351   496   523   471
   -71   -92   -70   -87   -82   -90

3. 239   452   567   422   565   463
   -48   -49   -49   -18   -49   -25

4. 344   475   621   643   476   438
   -28   -68   -19   -25   -27   -72

5. 571   582   563   434   473   565
   -90   -77   -81   -82   -91   -82

Subtract. Then put each letter in its matching blank to solve the puzzle.

Puzzle: What time is it when 10 hungry lions are chasing you? _____

6. 375   521   468   237   688   356   429
   -84   -60   -92   -86   -95   -71   -86
    T   E   O   F   R   A   N

   ___ ___ ___   ___ ___ ___ ___ ___   ___ ___ ___
   291 461 343   285 151 291 461 593   376 343 461

63

LESSON PLAN 9: A GAGGLE OF GREAT IDEAS

Here is an assortment of games, tricks and activities to help students master addition and subtraction.

1. FACTS OF THE WEEK

This can be run like a radio station contest. Fact or facts of the week are posted in a prominent place or written on the board. When students are away from the room or facing away from the poster, or the poster has been taken down, ask a student to give the fact or facts of the week. If the student answers correctly, he or she wins a coupon for a prize, page 69, to be collected just before dismissal.

FACTS OF THE WEEK
5 + 6 = 11
6 + 7 = 13
7 + 8 = 15
8 + 9 = 17

FACTS OF THE WEEK POSTER IDEAS:

(See page 68 for an example.) 8½" x 11" sheet of paper decorated with a border of stickers, wallpaper or art paper or a border printed from a computer program. The border could be seasonal. As a beginning of the year art project, let each student decorate one page and use a different page each week. Place the page in a vinyl page protector to reuse later this year or next year. Write the fact or facts with a dry-erase marker.

12" x 18" dry-erase board.

Tagboard or construction paper, laminated.

PRIZES:
Anything small and inexpensive such as candy, gum, pencils or a Free Homework pass. Don't use the free homework passes very often because students need to do homework for practice. Let students decorate homework passes and prize coupons. If you are going to give candy or gum, give it right before dismissal for the day. Ask parents to donate prizes.

DRAWING NAMES:
Start out the year with each student's name in a small container. When one student's name is drawn, put it in another container so that particular student cannot be drawn again until all others have had a chance. You could draw two or three each week or even one or more each day.

SUGGESTED FACTS TO USE:

Week 1: Double 5 + 5 through 10 + 10
Week 2: Number Neighbors—5 + 6 through 8 + 9
Week 3: Numbers Plus Nine—5 + 9 through 9 + 9
Week 4: A Number Family—for example, 5, 6, 11
5 + 6 = 11   11 - 5 = 6   11 - 6 = 5
Week 5: 4, 7, 11
Week 6: 3, 8, 11
Week 7: 4, 8, 12
Week 8: 5, 7, 12

Continue with number families or the more difficult addition and subtraction facts.

LESSON PLAN 9: CONTINUED

2. CALENDAR ADDITION AND SUBTRACTION
Worksheet Z, page 70

Show students the Base 10 Counting Chart (page 94). Since there are 10 numbers in each line, adding 10 to any number puts you directly below the starting number. A calendar page has seven numbers on each line, and if you add 7 to a number, the answer is just below the starting number. (Example: 8 + 7 = 15 and 15 is just below the 8 on a calendar.) When you subtract 7 from a number, you find the answer on a calendar page just above the starting number. (8 - 7 = 1)

Use old calendar pages or let students make their own calendar pages or copy an 8½" x 11" calendar page for each student.

GAME: For a quick and easy classroom game, call out a number, point to a student and the student must call out the answer to that number plus seven before the teacher can count to seven. Then the entire class chants that fact. (Example: Teacher calls out 6 and points to a student. Student must say 13 before teacher can count to 7. Then class says 6 + 7 = 13.) This could just be for a drill or the class could be divided into teams with scorekeeping. Let them use the calendar page for a few numbers and then try it with out the calendar.

3. NUMBER GROUPS FOR 10
Treasure Trove, Worksheet AA, page 71

When adding long columns of numbers, it is helpful to find pairs or groups of numbers that equal 10. The worksheet helps students learn number pairs for 10 and groups of numbers that equal 10. There are two sets of directions on the worksheet. Cover up the Directions (B) and run off the page the first time. Later, cover up the Directions (A) and run off the same page with more difficult directions.

4. HOPSCOTCH: ADDING AND SUBTRACTING 2 & 4

Copy the giant hopscotch numbers (pages 74-80). Place each page in a vinyl page protector and tape the pages together with clear vinyl tape. Leave a little space between each pair of page protectors so they can be folded accordion style. Use this in the classroom or at an outdoor recess. You could also draw large chalk numbers on cement outdoors.

For an indoor activity, give each student a small even and odd number line (page 73). Begin with adding two to an even number. (Review even and odd numbers in *Math Phonics*™–*Addition*, pages 20-27.)

Even number + 2 = jump to the next larger even number: 2 + 2 = 4

Even number - 2 = jump to the next smaller even number: 8 - 2 = 6

Even number + 4 = jump to the second larger even number: 6 + 4 = 10

Even number - 4 = jump to the second smaller even number: 12 - 4 = 8

For odd numbers, you are jumping back and forth on odd numbers.

Choose one student to hop on the large number line and call out the answer. Other students should have a small even and odd number line (page 73) and also find the answer. If they agree with the hopping student, they stand up. If not, they sit still and say nothing. Later they should be able to call out the answers without any number lines.

LESSON PLAN 9: CONTINUED

5. NINES GAME

Run off page 81 and cut apart the cards or make your own set on index cards cut in half. Be sure you have an even number of students so that each one has a partner. If you have an odd number of students, the teacher should play or have one student be the time keeper.

Pass out the cards, making sure each card has a match. Go over the nines addition facts, showing students how to mentally move one from the other number to the nine to make a group of 10. (See explanation entitled "Optional" at the end of page 43.)

When the time keeper says "go," students move quietly around the room looking for a matching card. When two students find that their cards match, they immediately sit down in two nearby desks. When the last pair of students matches, teacher calls "time" and time keeper writes the time on the board. Go over matching cards to see that students matched correctly. If anyone matched incorrectly, add five seconds for each mistake. Collect cards and pass them out again. When the class has reduced their time by 10 seconds, everyone gets a prize.

6. SUBTRACTION SOLITAIRE

Pages 82-86. One player game. This game can be made for each student to take home to play or each set of cards could be kept in a zip-type bag at school for students to use when they are finished with homework or during an indoor recess.

SOLITAIRE FOR 11: Run off two copies of page 82 on card stock. Cut the cards apart and mix thoroughly. Hold cards facedown and arrange as shown in the diagram.

LESSON PLAN 9: CONTINUED

Check to see if two cards in the bottom row match to form a subtraction fact for 11.

For example:

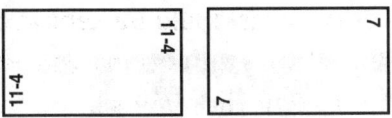

If so, remove the two matching cards and place them facedown to one side. Player holds remaining cards in hand and turns the first one face up. Check to see if it is a match with any other card which is completely uncovered. Students can use the facts chart for 11, page 25, if necessary or the Travel Folder for 11 in the *Math Phonics™–Subtraction* book, page 73. The object of the game is to match all cards faceup on the table. It is not necessary to match all cards in hand. This game is easy to win!

SOLITAIRE FOR 12: Make two copies of page 83 and play according to directions.

SOLITAIRE FOR 13: Make three copies of page 84 and play according to directions.

SOLITAIRE FOR 14 & 15: Make two copies of page 85 and follow directions.

SOLITAIRE FOR 16, 17 & 18: Make two copies of page 86 and follow directions.

Pages 81-86 can by used for a classroom matching game. Use the same rules as in the nines game.

7. DOUBLES & NUMBER NEIGHBORS FLASH CARDS

In the first book of *Math Phonics™–Addition*, doubles are used to help students learn number neighbors. (Refer to pages 28-43 in that book.) Some students catch on quickly and others do not. For those who do not, a set of flash cards is provided on pages 87-90 to help students learn number neighbors by thinking of doubles.

FACTS OF THE WEEK

$5 + 6 = 11$

$6 + 7 = 13$

$7 + 8 = 15$

$8 + 9 = 17$

HOMEWORK PASS	HOMEWORK PASS
HOMEWORK PASS	HOMEWORK PASS
PRIZE COUPON	PRIZE COUPON
PRIZE COUPON	PRIZE COUPON
PRIZE COUPON	PRIZE COUPON
PRIZE COUPON	PRIZE COUPON
PRIZE COUPON	PRIZE COUPON
PRIZE COUPON	PRIZE COUPON

Name _____   **WORKSHEET 2**

CALENDAR MATH

Use the calendar to help you answer these problems:

1	2	3	4	5	6	7
8	9	10	11	12	13	14
15	16					

1. 1   2   3   4   5   6   7   8   9
   +7 +7 +7 +7 +7 +7 +7 +7 +7

2. 8   9   10 11 12 13 14 15 16
   -7 -7 -7 -7 -7 -7 -7 -7 -7

- -

Fold on the dotted line and try the same problems without looking at the calendar.

3. 2   5   1   3   4   9   7   6   8
   +7 +7 +7 +7 +7 +7 +7 +7 +7

4. 11 8   10 9   16 12 15 13 14
   +7 +7 +7 +7 -7 -7 -7 -7 -7

5. 8   28 48 4   14 34 5   55 65
   +7 +7 +7 +7 +7 +7 +7 +7 +7

6. 6   16 36 3   23 43 9   29 49
   +7 +7 +7 +7 +7 +7 +7 +7 +7

7. 16 36 46 28 58 68 34 54 74
   +77 +77 +77 +77 +77 +77 +77 +77 +77

Name _____

TREASURE TROVE

WORKSHEET AA

The numbers on this treasure island represent piles of coins.

Directions (A): Circle pairs of numbers that equal 10. The numbers must be side-by-side, above and below or diagonal from each other. There cannot be another number between the two.

				1	3	4					
		2	7	9	3	2	4	5	2		
1	5	8	3	4	1	5	3	6	3	8	
9	4	5	3	3	2	3	8	2	4	2	
2	1	1	2	3	4	1	3	2	5	3	1
6	8	2	7	1	9	6	2	5	1	7	2
5	1	1	1	2	7	3	1	9	2	2	5
5	3	9	4	9	1	7	2	1	3	7	1
	2	6	5	6	3	7	5	6	5	5	8
	3	5	3	1	3	3	3	3	4	1	
	4	5	5	2	4	2	4	2		6	
	1	2	3		4	1	5	8			

Directions (B): Circle groups of 3, 4 or 5 numbers that equal 10. Numbers must be side-by-side, above and below or diagonal from each other. There cannot be another number inbetween the numbers.

71

Name _____   WORKSHEET BB

ADDING & SUBTRACTING 2s & 4s

2	4	6	8	1	3
+2	+2	+2	+2	+2	+2

5	7	9	2	4	6
+2	+2	+2	+4	+4	+4

8	1	3	5	7	9
+4	+4	+4	+4	+4	+4

10	8	6	4	11	9
-2	-2	-2	-2	-2	-2

7	5	3	12	22	34
-2	-2	-2	+2	+4	+22

45	54	65	76	87	98
+44	-22	-44	-22	-44	-22

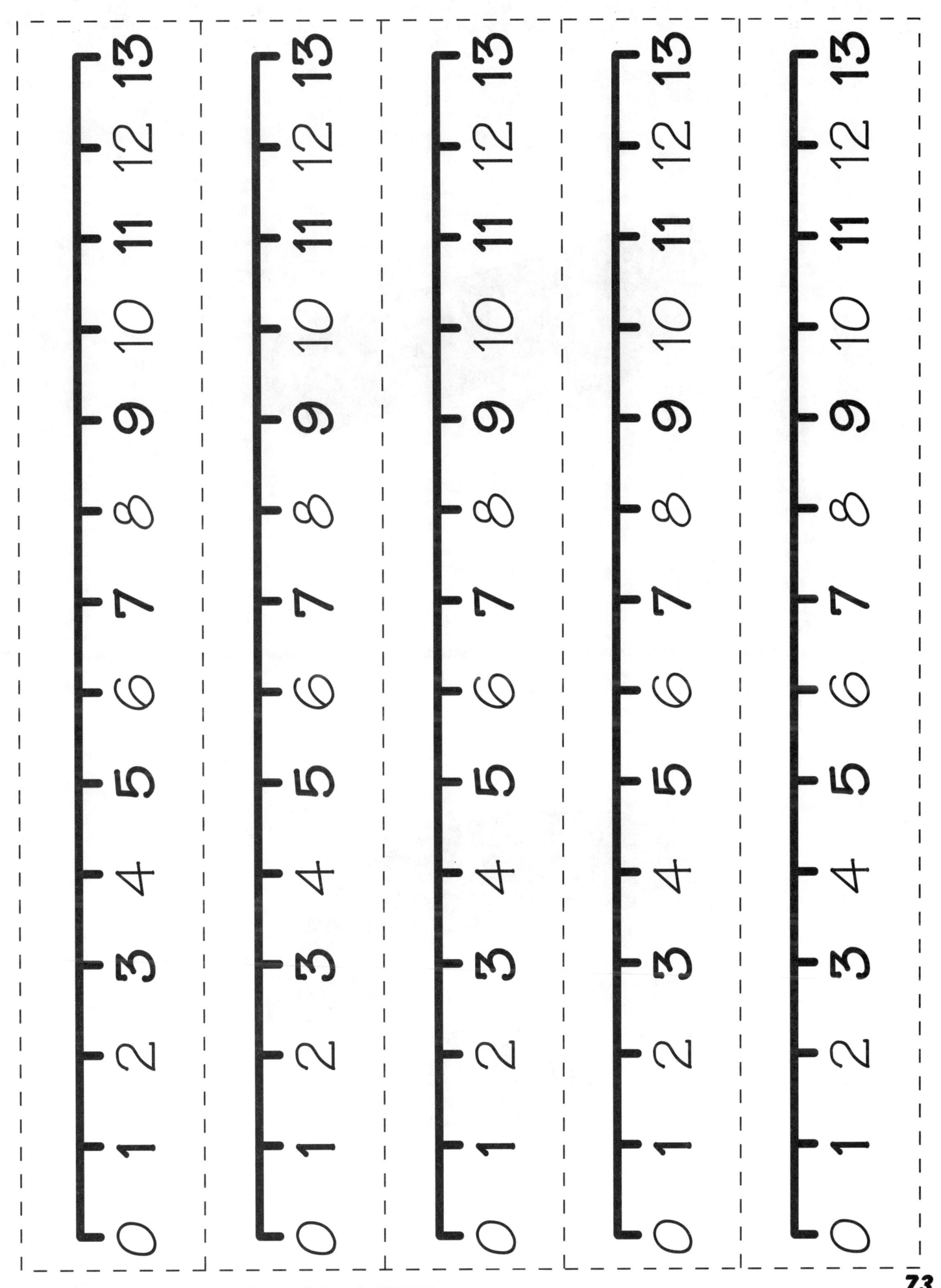

75

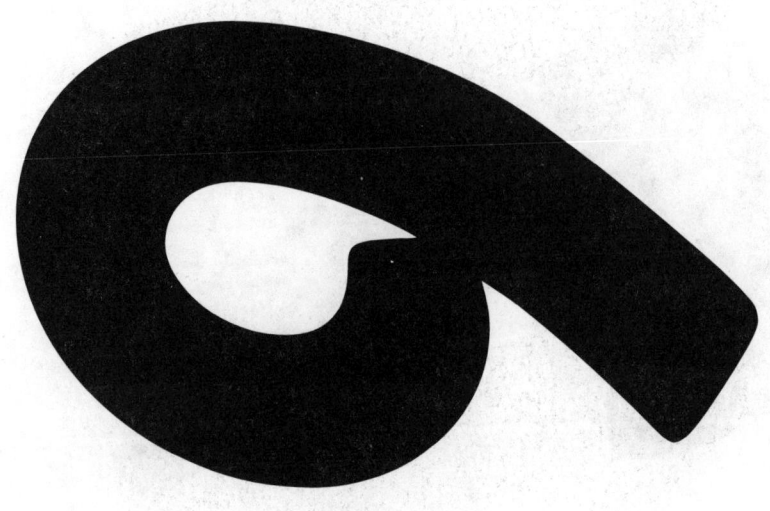

18	9 + 9	18	9 + 9
17	9 + 8	17	9 + 8
16	9 + 7	16	9 + 7
15	9 + 6	15	9 + 6
14	9 + 5	14	9 + 5
13	9 + 4	13	9 + 4
12	9 + 3	12	9 + 3
11	9 + 2	11	9 + 2

11-2	11-3	11-4	11-5	11-6
11-7	11-8	11-9	2	3
4	5	6	7	8
9				

82 Make two copies.

12-3	12-4	12-5	12-6	12-7
12-3	12-4	12-5	12-6	12-7
12-8	12-9	3	4	5
12-8	12-9	3	4	5
6	7	8	9	
6	7	8	9	

Make two copies.

13-4	13-5	13-6	13-7	13-8
13-9	4	5	<u>6</u>	7
8	<u>9</u>			

14-5	14-6	14-7	14-8	14-9
14-5	14-6	14-7	14-8	14-9
5	6	7	8	9
5	6	7	8	9
15-6	15-7	15-8	15-9	6
15-6	15-7	15-8	15-9	6
7	8	9		
7	8	9		

16-7 / 16-7	16-8 / 16-8	16-9 / 16-9	7 / 7	8 / 8
9 / 9	17-8 / 17-8	17-9 / 17-9	8 / 8	9 / 9
16-7 / 16-7	16-8 / 16-8	16-9 / 16-9	7 / 7	8 / 8
9 / 9	17-8 / 17-8	9 / 9	18-9 / 18-9	9 / 9

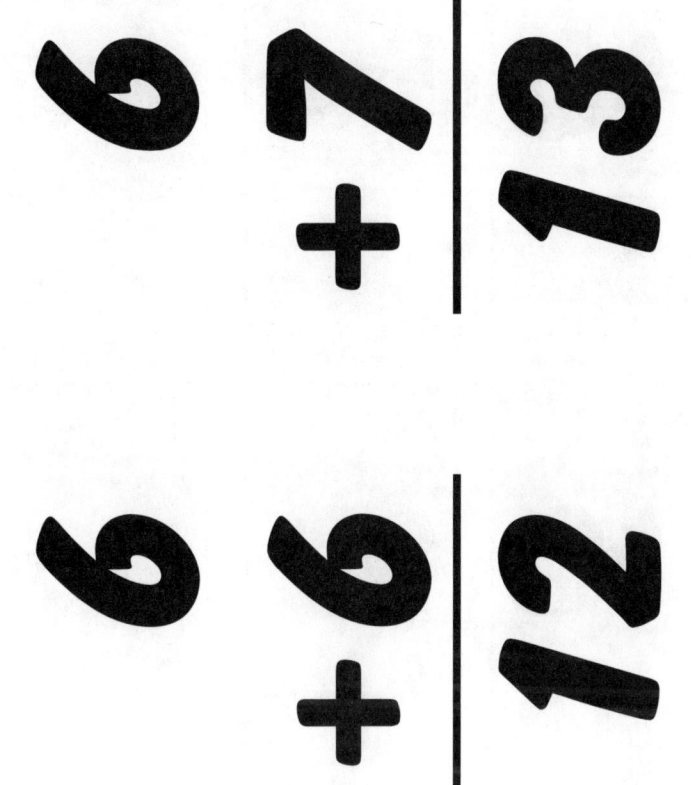

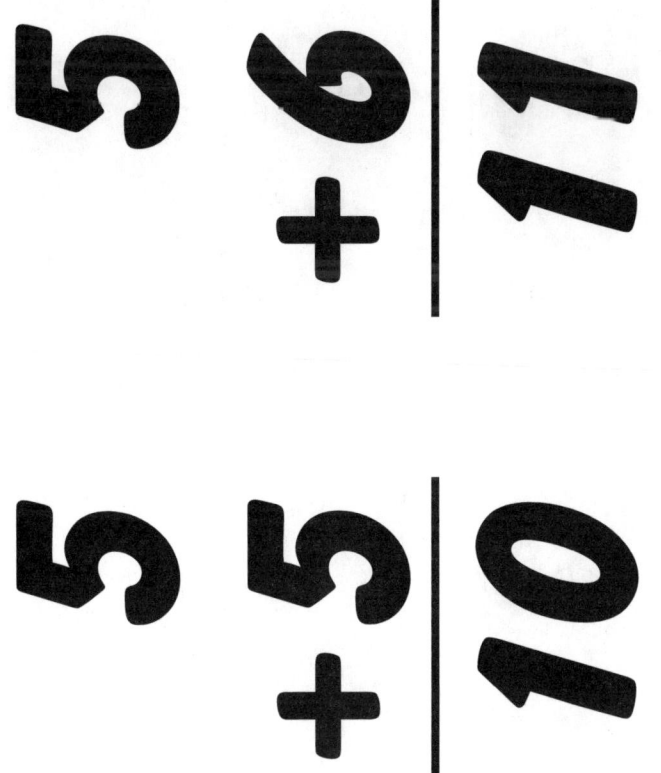

```
  6      6      5     5
+ 7    + 6    + 6   + 5
```

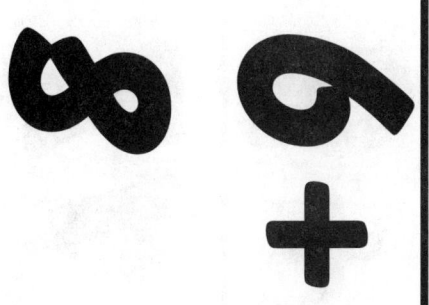

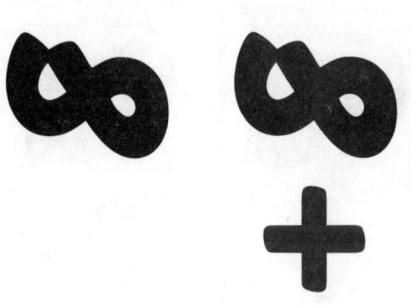

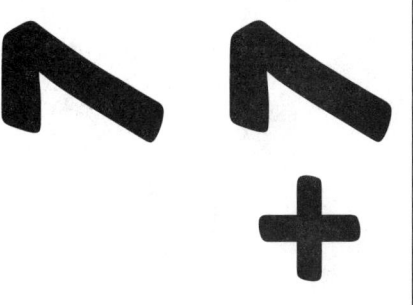

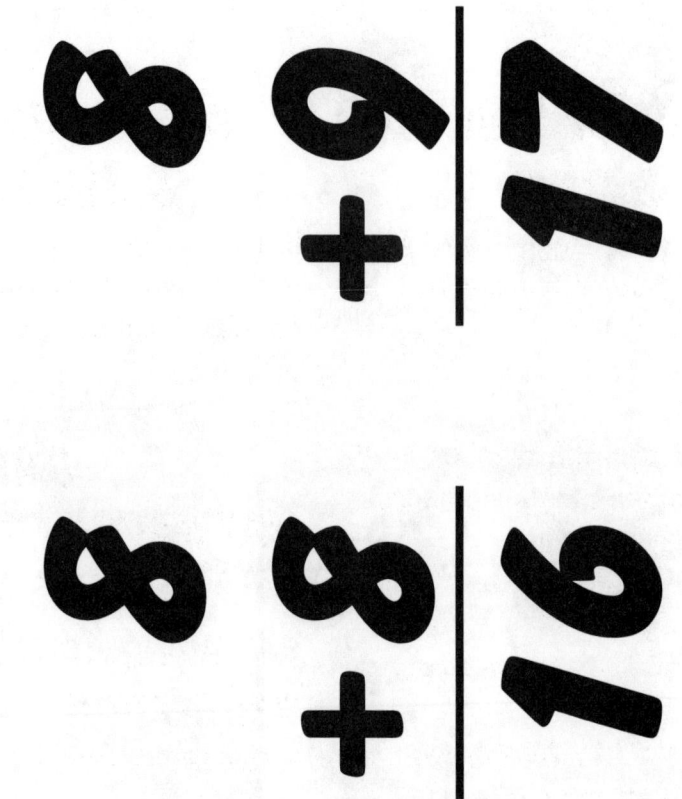
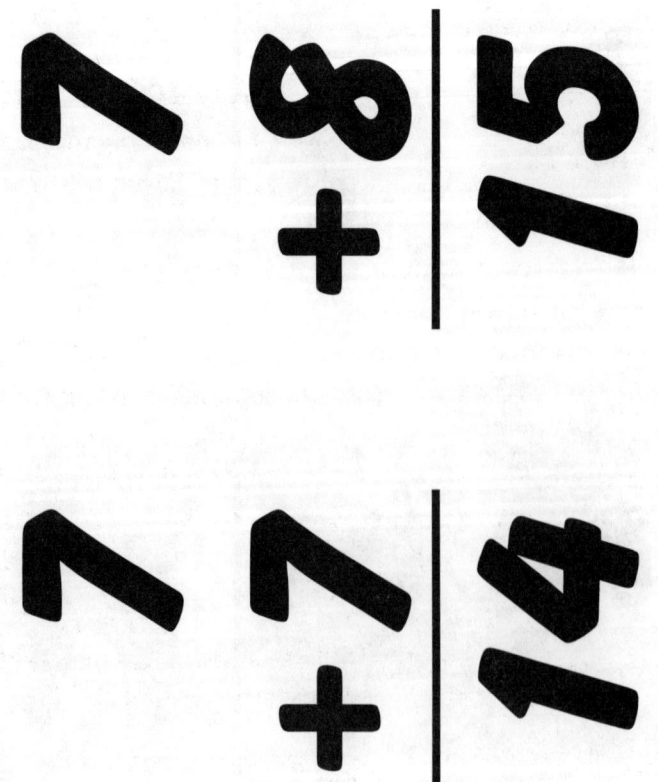

LESSON PLAN 10: RULES, GAMES & ASSESSMENTS

RULES FOR ADDITION NUMBER PAIRS

A. For number pairs for sums larger than 10, the first number pair is some number plus 10. Name the 10 second.
Example: 1 + 10 = 11

B. For the next number pair, the number in the first column gets larger and the number in the second column gets smaller.
Example: 1 + 10 = 11
2 + 9 = 11
3 + 8 = 11 and so on.

C. Find these number pairs by moving two index fingers toward the center of a ruler. In this rainbow diagram, pairs of number which equal 11 are joined by curved lines:

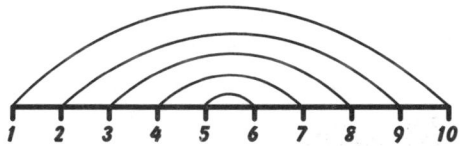

SUBTRACTION NUMBER PAIRS

For each addition fact, make one or two subtraction facts from the same three numbers. Use a mini facts chart (page 25 or 27) to find unknown subtraction answers.
Example:
2 + 9 = 11   5 + 5 = 10
11 - 2 = 9   10 - 5 = 5
11 - 9 = 2

CALENDAR ADDITION & SUBTRACTION

Pick a number on a calendar (Example: 8). The number directly below the 8 equals 8 + 7 or 15. The number directly above the 8 is 8 - 7 or 1.

GAMES

SUBTRACTION STEPPING-STONES
Page 50. Directions page 47.

CALENDAR ADDITION & SUBTRACTION
Verbal game. Page 65.

HOPSCOTCH
Adding and subtracting 2 and 4. Page 65.

NINES GAME
Classroom card matching game. Page 66.

SUBTRACTION SOLITAIRE
One person game or classroom card matching game. Pages 66-67.

Assessments in this book are on pages 92 and 93. Also, find assessments in *Math Phonics*™– *Addition*, page 89 and *Math Phonics*™– *Subtraction*, pages 93 and 94. For achievement certificates, *Math Phonics*™–*Addition*, page 90 and *Math Phonics*™–*Subtraction* page 96.

Name _____   **ASSESSMENT**

ADDITION & SUBTRACTION 11-18

1.   6   5   7   9   6
     +6   +6   +9   +9   +7

2.   8   6   4   7   9
     +6   +9   +7   +5   +5

3.   7   8   5   3   8
     +8   +4   +8   +8   +8

4.   9   8   4   7   2
     +3   +9   +9   +7   +9

5. 14   15   11   12   13   11
     -5   -7   -2   -9   -5   -6

6. 11   12   14   11   12   13
     -7   -6   -6   -3   -8   -4

7. 13   11   12   14   11   12
     -9   -8   -5   -7   -4   -7

8. 16   13   11   12   14   11
     -7   -8   -9   -4   -8   -5

9. 14   15   13   16   12   15
     -9   -9   -7   -8   -3   -8

10. 15   17   17   13   16   18
     -6   -8   -9   -6   -9   -9

Name _____   **ASSESSMENT**

ADDITION & SUBTRACTION

1.	24 +7	54 +8	27 +9	66 +8	49 +2
2.	29 +49	37 +27	49 +23	67 +26	57 +25
3.	136 +255	238 +438	369 +228	128 +357	526 +349
4.	165 +429	207 +386	348 +125	139 +204	423 +318
5.	64 -15	75 -27	41 -12	72 -29	73 -35	61 -16
6.	51 -37	82 -36	34 -16	61 -23	92 -58	23 -14
7.	73 -49	71 -38	32 -15	84 -27	31 -14	42 -27
8.	286 -37	443 -28	341 -39	672 -54	594 -68	381 -45
9.	348 -92	457 -94	536 -72	669 -84	425 -32	358 -87
10.	556 -63	477 -81	679 -94	338 -65	765 -91	685 -94

BASE 10 COUNTING CHART

1	2	3	4	5	6	7	8	9	10
11	12	13	14	15	16	17	18	19	20
21	22	23	24	25	26	27	28	29	30
31	32	33	34	35	36	37	38	39	40
41	42	43	44	45	46	47	48	49	50
51	52	53	54	55	56	57	58	59	60
61	62	63	64	65	66	67	68	69	70
71	72	73	74	75	76	77	78	79	80
81	82	83	84	85	86	87	88	89	90
91	92	93	94	95	96	97	98	99	100
101	102	103	104	105	106	107	108	109	110
111	112	113	114	115	116	117	118	119	120
121	122	123	124	125	126	127	128	129	130
131	132	133	134	135	136	137	138	139	140
141	142	143	144	145	146	147	148	149	150

ANSWER KEY

Worksheet A, page 14
Challenge: Some might be today's date, price of paper, temperature, page numbers, KGE rate increase (and other news story details), percent of workers being laid off, length and weight of a new baby, distance in miles between two cities, number of years a factory has existed, gasoline prices, number of Americans traveling over a holiday weekend and many more! (You could also ask students to write down the actual numbers.)

Worksheet B, page 15
1. 11, 31, 41, 61, 11, 41, 71, 91   2. 11, 31, 61, 91, 11, 51, 81, 91
3. 12, 42, 52, 62, 12, 32, 52, 72   4. 12, 32, 52, 92, 12, 62, 82, 92

Number Pairs—
1 + 10 = 11	2 + 10 = 12	3 + 10 = 13	4 + 10 = 14
2 + 9 = 11	3 + 9 = 12	4 + 9 = 13	5 + 9 = 14
3 + 8 = 11	4 + 8 = 12	5 + 8 = 13	6 + 8 = 14
4 + 7 = 11	5 + 7 = 12	6 + 7 = 13	7 + 7 = 14
5 + 6 = 11	6 + 6 = 12		

5. 31 pens   6. 21 boxes
Challenge: 4

Worksheet C, page 16
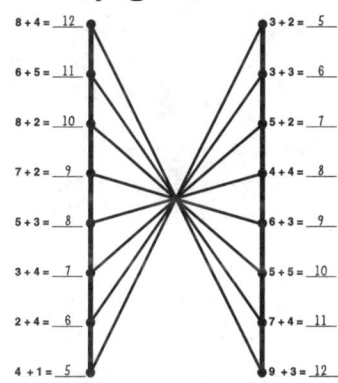

Worksheet D, page 20
Challenge: 6☆ = 12, 10☆ = 16. Star process adds 6 to a number.

Worksheet E, page 21
1. 13, 33, 63, 93, 13, 23, 53, 83   2. 13, 43, 73, 93, 14, 34, 54, 84
3. 14, 34, 54, 74, 14, 44, 74, 84   4. 12, 11, 11, 12, 11, 12, 11, 12
5. 13, 14, 11, 12, 11, 12, 11, 12   6. $23   7. 21 boxes
Challenge: 15
6	1	8
7	5	3
2	9	4

Worksheet F, page 22
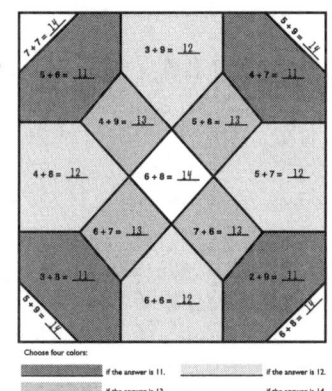

Worksheet G, page 32
Challenge: 7

Worksheet H, page 33
1. 15, 45, 75, 95, 15, 55, 75, 85   2. 16, 56, 86, 96, 16, 66, 66, 96
3. 17, 67, 87, 97, 18, 48, 78, 98   4. 11, 14, 11, 12, 12, 11, 11, 14
5. 13, 12, 13, 14, 14, 13, 13, 12   6. $37   7. 21 hours
Challenge: 9999; 9876

Worksheet I, page 34
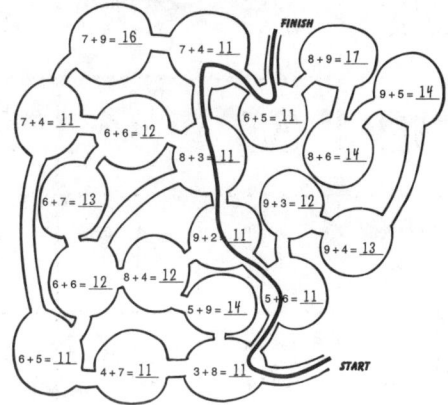

Worksheet J, page 41
1. 11, 15, 14, 12, 17, 17, 13   2. 16, 16, 12, 11, 12, 15, 16
3. 13, 12, 15, 14, 13, 11, 11   4. 11, 14, 16, 14, 12, 18, 13
5. 10, 8, 5, 6, 8, 9, 10, 7   6. 4, 7, 8, 10, 9, 6, 10, 9
7. 31, 47, 62, 36, 74, 85, 51, 60   8. 99, 109, 52, 78, 96, 84, 72, 93
9. 81, 80, 82, 75, 91, 60, 76, 82

Worksheet K, page 41
Challenge: 29

Worksheet L, page 42
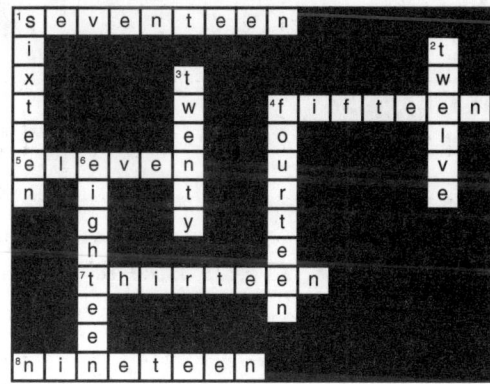

Worksheet M, page 44
Challenge: 133
            525
          +21[3]
          [8]71

Worksheet N, page 45
Challenge: one

ANSWER KEY

Worksheet O, page 46

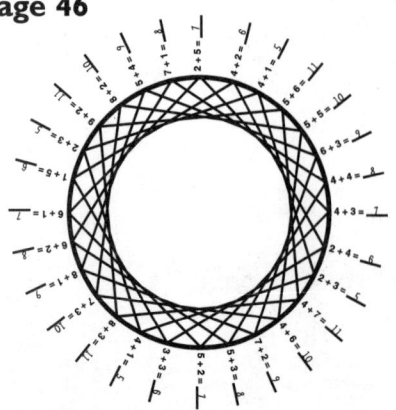

Worksheet P, page 48
Challenge: 1234

Worksheet Q, page 49
Challenge: 603

Worksheet R, page 52
Number Pairs—
5 + 10   6 + 10   7 + 10   8 + 10
6 + 9   7 + 9   8 + 9   9 + 9
7 + 8   8 + 8

1. 9, 8, 7, 9, 8   2. 6, 7, 9, 9, 8   3. 45, 75, 75, 66, 66, 35, 75
4. 56, 76, 96, 57, 67, 68, 98   5. 8 feet   6. $9 more
Challenge: Jan took first; Joan took second; Gene took third; John won fourth place.

Worksheet S, page 53
1. 8, 8, 7, 7, 9, 7, 8   2. 9, 9, 6, 8, 8, 9, 7
3. 396, 666, 597, 486, 875, 895, 575
4. 597, 594, 585, 735, 686, 566, 545
5. 593, 473, 742, 482, 394, 343, 384
6. $7   7. ribbons—$7
Challenge: 2, 3, 4, 5, 6, 7, 8, 9, one more

Worksheet T, page 54
The answer at the top should always be 2.

Worksheet V, page 60
1. 28, 38, 48, 47, 57, 67, 27, 37, 47   2. 19, 39, 59, 38, 48, 58, 5, 25, 45
3. 25, 45, 65, 37, 47, 57, 17, 27, 37   4. 23, 33, 43, 18, 38, 58, 18, 28, 38   5. 19, 29, 39, 19, 39, 59, 19, 29, 39   6. 17, 27, 37, 16, 26, 36, 14, 24, 34   7. 36 people   8. $39
Challenge: Sunday = $128; total = $254

Worksheet W, page 61
1. 37, 59, 64, 19, 44, 15, 56   2. 29, 74, 19, 52, 28, 17, 18
3. 27, 38, 34, 44, 66, 49, 47   4. 35, 28, 24, 16, 33, 27, 37
5. 29, 15, 10, 26, 29, 27, 56   6. 39, 48, 49, 22, 26, 27, 28
7. 18 pounds   8. 27 more cans of fruit
Challenge: Example: Choose 6 as the first number; second number is 60. Second minus first is 60 - 6 = 54. Add nine, 54 + 9 = 63. Add the two numerals, 6 + 3 = 9. The answer is always 9!

Worksheet X, page 62
1. 71, 191, 281, 74, 184, 262   2. 61, 162, 264, 81, 181, 282
3. 92, 182, 281, 83, 190, 294   4. 141, 257, 363, 93, 191, 293
5. 194, 294, 355, 67, 151, 343
Puzzle: envelope

Worksheet Y, page 63
1. 249, 107, 191, 281, 341, 181   2. 452, 394, 281, 409, 441, 381
3. 191, 403, 518, 404, 516, 438   4. 316, 407, 602, 618, 449, 366
5. 481, 505, 482, 352, 382, 483
Puzzle: ten after one

Worksheet Z, page 70
1. 8, 9, 10, 11, 12, 13, 14, 15, 16   2. 1, 2, 3, 4, 5, 6, 7, 8, 9
3. 9, 12, 8, 10, 11, 16, 14, 13, 15   4. 18, 15, 17, 16, 9, 5, 8, 6, 7
5. 15, 35, 55, 11, 21, 41, 12, 62, 72   6. 13, 23, 43, 10, 30, 50, 16, 36, 56
7. 93, 113, 123, 105, 135, 145, 111, 131, 151

Worksheet AA, page 71
Directions A:

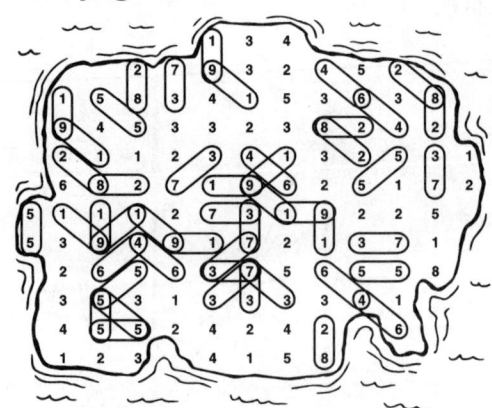

Directions B:

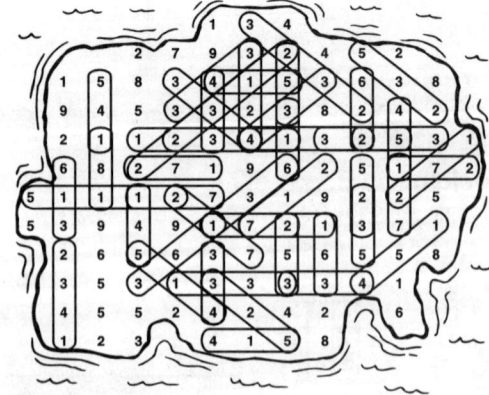

Worksheet BB, page 72
1. 4, 6, 8, 10, 3, 5   2. 7, 9, 11, 6, 8, 10   3. 12, 5, 7, 9, 11, 13
4. 8, 6, 4, 2, 9, 7   5. 5, 3, 1, 14, 26, 56   6. 89, 32, 21, 54, 43, 76

Assessment, page 93
1. 31, 62, 36, 74, 51   2. 78, 84, 72, 93, 82
3. 391, 676, 597, 485, 875   4. 594, 593, 473, 343, 741
5. 49, 48, 29, 43, 38, 45   6. 14, 46, 18, 38, 34, 9
7. 24, 33, 17, 57, 17, 15   8. 249, 415, 302, 618, 526, 336
9. 256, 363, 464, 585, 393, 271   10. 493, 396, 585, 273, 674, 591

SCIENCE FUN

Activities to Encourage Students to Think and Solve Problems

Written by Edward Shevick
Illustrated by Marguerite Jones

Teaching & Learning Company

1204 Buchanan St., P.O. Box 10
Carthage, IL 62321-0010

This book belongs to

_____

The activity portrayed on the front cover is described on pages 9-10.

Cover design by Kelly Bollin

Copyright © 1998, Teaching & Learning Company

ISBN No. 1-57310-140-0

Printing No. 987654321

Teaching & Learning Company
1204 Buchanan St., P.O. Box 10
Carthage, IL 62321-0010

The purchase of this book entitles teachers to make copies for use in their individual classrooms only. This book, or any part of it, may not be reproduced in any form for any other purposes without prior written permission from the Teaching & Learning Company. It is strictly prohibited to reproduce any part of this book for an entire school or school district, or for commercial resale.

All rights reserved. Printed in the United States of America.